THE YOGA OF LOVE

JAMES SWARTZ

ISBN 978-1-329-94985-0

Cover design: ©James Swartz

Sculpture: ©Isabella Viglietti

Contents

Foreword

WHEN I STARTED commentaries on Vedanta in the nineties, the first text I tackled was *Atma Bodh,* an introductory treatise on self-knowledge. I commented on *Narada Bhakti Sutras* next because success is not possible unless the head and the heart work together. My experience teaching Western people convinced me that although they had little trouble understanding the basic knowledge, their emotional lives left something to be desired, owing to their long-standing immersion in materialism. We experience emotional problems for at least two reasons: abuse and neglect as children owing to the breakdown of the extended family and lack of access to an intelligent religion capable of sublimating dysfunctional emotions into a positive devotional life, leading to self-inquiry, freedom and non-dual love. The subtitle of my first commentaries on the *sutras,* "The Logic of Love," is not an oxymoron, because knowledge and love are one.

The word "religion" comes from the Latin word *religare,* which means "to bind" or "to connect." A ligament connects two bones. Religion "reconnects" the individual "back" to God, implying a severed connection. The word "*yoga*" in the title of these commentaries connects the reflected self, the "soul," to use religious terminology, back to God, pure original consciousness/existence/love, setting it free of its bondage to the body and the material world.

Vedanta is a means of self-knowledge that leads to freedom and non-dual love, so it is not a religion. However, it does not reject the religious impulse, one of man's most notable, noble and all-pervasive tendencies. Instead, it seeks to inform this impulse with deep understanding.

The *Bhakti Sutras* are verses by a great sage, Narada, on the topic of love. I was always attracted to them and had heard them unfolded at the feet of my teacher, Swami Chinmayananda, in 1969. Unfortunately, I only had an English translation from Swami Prabhavananda with the typical quasi-Vedic slant of the Ramakrishna Mission, which was helpful but not ideal. I wasn't a very good writer then, so my ability to communicate Vedanta was not as sophisticated as it is today. I always intended to improve the commentaries, but one thing led to another and it never happened.

In the meantime, the internet happened, my writing improved and my books and commentaries began to attract an international readership. Early this year I learned of audio talks of the *sutras* by Swami Paramarthananda, a *guru* brother and the foremost disciple of the great sage Swami Dayananda Saraswati, one of my teachers. My ShiningWorld duties, a hectic schedule of international travel and work on my most recent book, *Inquiry into Existence,* commentaries on Vidyaranya's *Panchadasi,* prevented me from listening to the Swami's excellent talks. Fortunately, a young woman named Luma Muhtadie offered to transcribe them and did an excellent job. I finished *Inquiry into Existence,* and with the help of the Swami's talks have, I feel, done justice to this important work.

It is an important text, not only because Western seekers generally have love problems that Indian devotees avoid, owing to the pervasiveness of India's devotional culture, but because the many erroneous notions of devotion and liberation floating around in the spiritual world need to be properly contextualized to help devotees, East and West, achieve non-dual love.

It is also important because seekers need to know the benefit of self-inquiry: how Vedanta will transform them and their lives. The *sutras* give us an excellent picture of a self-actualized person, someone who enjoys complete freedom and non-dual love.

Finally, these days we see many self-proclaimed "enlightened" people professing to be free. Generally, this freedom is left undefined or amounts to freedom from social constraints and/or one's conditioning, which, depending on how you look at it, is not necessarily the kiss of death. However, I am not aware of any modern teaching that conflates liberation with non-dual (unconditional) love, which might fairly be said to be the next step after enlightenment. If Vedanta's definition of liberation (*moksa*) were adhered to, the number of "enlightened beings" would shrink to imperceptibility and the many abuses visited on seekers by modern teachers would virtually disappear. In any case, these *sutras* are the last word on freedom and non-dual love.

I dedicate this book to my darling wife, Sundari, who is an embodiment of pure love and who created the sculpture for our fourth wedding anniversary that appears on the cover of this book.

Bend, Oregon, December 25, 2015

Introduction

THE WORD "*BHAKTI*" is generally translated as "devotion" and is reverential love directed toward God. God is one's self plus all the objects, sentient and insentient, in the world. Devotion is an important topic for inquirers, as it is a key qualification for attaining self-knowledge, the hard and fast understanding that one's nature is pure love. Assimilated self-knowledge is liberation (*moksa*), freedom from dependence on objects. In devotional language, liberation means freedom from the need to love objects – mainly people – and consequently complete love of one's self, limitless awareness, the nature of which is love. Because the limited self, the person, is an object in awareness, love of the self includes unconditional love of the personal self, the ego. Self-knowledge leads to the hard and fast realization that one's nature is pure love. Love is perhaps the topic dearest to us because anyone who does not have it wants it, those who have it want more of it and are always terrified of losing it.

As it says in verse 6.23 of the *Svetashvatara Upanishad,* one of the source texts on the topic of devotion:

> "Only those great souls who have intense devotion for God and equal devotion to the teacher of self-knowledge will fully comprehend the teachings of Vedanta."

Likewise, toward the end of the eighteenth chapter of the *Bhagavad Gita* (verse 18.67), Vedanta's most important scripture on liberation, action and devotion, says, "This teaching should never be imparted to one who is devoid of discipline and the spirit of renunciation, nor to one who is not devoted to God, nor to one who is not desirous of hearing the teachings of Vedanta and the glories of the Lord, nor to one who is doubtful about the existence of the self."

The topic of devotion is elaborated upon in the *Puranas, Itihasas* and *Agamas,*[1] especially the *Puranas,* which go into great detail about the exploits of the Lord,

[1]*Puranas* are ancient Hindu texts eulogizing various deities, primarily the Trimurti (i.e. Brahma, Vishnu and Shiva), in story form. *Itihasas* are epic histories, principally the *Ramayana* and *Mahabharata. Agamas* are non-Vedic scriptures dealing with the spiritual philosophy and practices behind deity worship.

the glories of the Lord and the greatness of great devotees. In these texts the self, limitless, non-dual, impersonal, all-pervasive, ever-present consciousness, appears as a free person living in the world, an emanation of the Divine, who is not separate from it. Vedanta says that one method of acquiring, nourishing and stoking devotion is through exposure to the biographies of saintly devotees. Accordingly, there is a vast literature on the lives of great devotees.

What Is a Devotee?

All individuals (*jivas*) are devotees whether they know it or not. This is because individuals are not self-created. They are created by God. God is existence and every object in it. Because of this fact the individual is completely dependent on God. Non-believers that object to the word "God" do not think of themselves as devotees, but they are devotees nonetheless because although they love God's stuff, they actually love God because God's stuff is non-separate from God. In this text, a devotee is someone who recognizes his or her dependence on God and either wants God's stuff, knowledge of God or non-separation from God.

A devotee is always in conflict because the self, which is ever-free, creates a constant desire for freedom in his heart which conflicts with his conditioning, which in turn trains him to love changing objects: people, things and situations. When the desire for freedom becomes so troublesome that it can no longer be ignored, he consciously becomes a devotee and begins the arduous transference of love for unreliable objects to the ever-present, unchanging and ever-reliable self, the life principle in the form of God, the creator of all things and the deliverer of the results of his actions.

By studying the biographies of famous devotees, we learn about various devotional exercises, such as listening to the teachings of the *Vedas*, chanting the Lord's name, remembering the Lord, serving the Lord, ritual worship, or *puja*, prostrating to the Lord, cultivating virtuous qualities and so forth. We also learn about varieties of relationships with the Lord, which might be called styles of worship. Countless stories, poems and songs have been composed about these various relationships, resulting in a vast literature. This type of devotion is also very media-friendly, hence its popularity.

Love and Knowledge

As a consequence of the ubiquity and popularity of the devotional literature, misunderstandings about devotion abound. Though widespread exposure to devotional culture is wonderful on the one hand, it brings unnecessary problems which are rarely discussed among non-inquirers, but must be eventually addressed by serious seekers. In general, the entire body of devotional literature deals with two topics. The first is devotional practice (*sadhana*) and encompasses forms of devotional relationship, devotional exercises and values. Secondly, the devotional literature talks about the highest goal of life, liberation, and the relationship between devotion and liberation.

When we take up the topic of liberation we enter into the philosophical domain, where different points of view obtain. And although Vedanta is not a philosophy or a point of view – it is simply a common-sense means of self-knowledge, which is tantamount to liberation – it looks like a philosophy to the uninitiated. So to avoid argumentation on this topic and to expose illogical and irrational views with reference to liberation, we provisionally accept the idea that Vedanta is a philosophy or a point of view, a *darshana*. We might fairly call the *Narada Bhakti Sutras* the "philosophy" of divine love.

Serious seekers of liberation who are committed to self-inquiry in the form of Vedanta need to know that while devotional practices are useful, the basic point of view of devotional literature is not useful, because it is not non-dual; it sees an eternal separation between the devotee and the Lord, which Vedanta completely rejects. There is even a verse from the *Bhagavata Purana*, the Bible of the *bhaktas* (devotees), that says, "I am not even interested in liberation (*moksa*), I want to enjoy devotion of you, Lord, as my personal god." Thus, like the Yoga *darshana*, the philosophy of devotion is anti-Vedic. Whereas *yoga* practice is wonderful because it neutralizes pesky worldly tendencies (*vasanas*), the ideas of Yoga about liberation are illogical and nonsensical, and should be rejected because they are based on the heterodox view that reality is a duality. Indeed the *Brahma Sutras*, one of the three pillars of Vedanta, are a systematic analysis and dismissal of various philosophical arguments that contradict the non-dual point of view. To be more specific, the devotional *darshana* directly contravenes Vedantic inquiry, whose cornerstone is hearing (*sruti*), reasoning (*yukti*) and experiential assimilation (*anubhava*[2]).

[2] *Sruti* refers to scriptural authority and corresponds to *sravana*, or listening. *Yukti* refers to logic and reasoning and corresponds to *manana*, which involves reflecting deeply upon the scripture-based teaching that was heard and resolving any and all doubts. *Anubhava* is literally translated as "experience," but this translation leaves a lot to be desired. In certain context, including the present one, *anubhava* means "direct knowledge." *Anubhava* corresponds to *nididhyasana*, assimilating self-knowledge until it becomes unshakable.

Therefore when we study devotional literature – although this text is an exception – we need to discriminate the practices, which are valuable, from the ideas, which are not – assuming an individual wants freedom, which is non-dual love. Non-dual love is the solution to one of the world's signature problems: loneliness and separation. People feel lonely and expect love relationships to set them free, which they do momentarily, but which soon enough bind the lover to the love object, the antithesis of freedom. Love relationships aside, if you look deeper you discover that when you get what you want you are satisfied with yourself, which means that you actually love yourself. If you didn't love yourself, you wouldn't waste your time trying to satisfy yourself. When you love yourself, you are adequate to deal with anything life has to offer; you are confident. In these moments of freedom your mind is resolved, and a resolved mind, untroubled by desire and fear, experiences the fullness/love that is its nature.

Provisional Acceptance of Duality

Just as we provisionally accept the idea that Vedanta is a philosophy, we also provisionally accept the devotional *darshana's* view that the apparent duality between the devotee and God is an actual duality because it is instrumental for emotional purification and for expanding our intellectual understanding of the nature of reality. Acceptance of permanent duality is a problem because it causes continual suffering. If the devotional *darshana* is the opposing view, what is the real view? The answer is established in the three authoritative texts of Vedanta – the *Upanishads,* the *Bhagavad Gita* and the *Brahma Sutras* – which adhere to the threefold yardstick of hearing, reasoning and assimilation, and have been carefully preserved and perpetuated by an exceptional *guru*-student lineage. Keeping the four fundamental principles of the Vedantic view in mind serves as our best filter when studying devotional literature.

The Four Fundamentals

1. Liberation is the highest goal[3] of human life. It is synonymous with non-dual love.

2. It can only be accomplished by self-knowledge because we are already free. What exactly is that knowledge? *Brahma satyam, jagan mithya, jivo brahmaiva na aparah* – the self alone is real, the universe is apparently real: the individual is non-different from the self. Knowledge is not entertaining

a conceptual understanding of this phrase; it is enjoying a direct, fully assimilated and unshakable conviction of the underlying truth that it expresses.

3. Self-knowledge does not happen automatically and is only accomplished by Vedantic inquiry: listening, reasoning and assimilating under the guidance of a proper *guru.*

4. Inquiry is only possible if the mind is refined. This refinement is accomplished through *karma yoga* and *upasana yoga,*[4] both of which require dualistic devotion to God.

Karma yoga requires dualistic devotion because the devotee reverentially dedicates every single action, mundane and spiritual, to the Lord. *Upasana yoga* requires dualistic devotion because the devotee/inquirer dwells reverentially upon the Lord as an object of worship. But whereas devotional philosophy would have us retain this duality permanently, Vedanta ushers the devotee through the sacred portals of inquiry, which is a more refined form of dualistic devotion and which in turn culminates in non-dual devotion, the end of separation and seeking and the constant appreciation of the ever-present experience of non-dual love, the ultimate aim of human life.

Four Features of Informal Dualistic Devotion

Devotional literature can be useful insofar as it can inform the practice of *karma yoga* and *upasana yoga.* It enjoys certain beneficial features not found in the *Vedas* and constitutes what might be called informal dualistic devotion.

1. The first feature is that God (*Isvara*) is brought down to the human level, which is contrary to Vedanta's goal, raising the mind up to *Isvara's* level and beyond to the level of pure uncreated consciousness. Going beyond God is not a blasphemous idea, because the devotee rediscovers an identity that includes both God and the individual and conflicts with neither. There is no conflict, because God and the individual are in one order of reality, and the self, pure love/consciousness, is in another.

[3]According to Vedanta, all human goals can be reduced to four types: (1) *artha,* or security, (2) *kama,* or pleasure, (3) *dharma,* or virtue, and (4) *moksa,* or liberation. The pursuit of *artha, kama* and *dharma* is a permanent struggle. With *moksa* all struggle ends because one discovers security and joy in oneself. Thus the four can be reduced to two: *artha-kama-dharma,* the pursuit of ever-changing, apparently real objects, and *moksa,* the pursuit of the unchanging real self.

[4]*Upasana yoga* is meditation and self-inquiry.

2. In any case, looking at the reality from the individual's point of view, once God has been humanized, a relationship amenable to a wide range of possibilities is struck with the personified God. For example, drawing from the library of human emotional archetypes, God may be treated as a mother, father, baby, a lover, a master or a parent.

3. The third feature is that after striking up this relationship with a humanized God, regular and intimate interaction unconfined by prescribed rules takes place. The devotee interacts with God at any time, in any place and in any manner he or she pleases. God can be cuddled and pinched, kissed and caressed, cried to, confided in and even scolded – and all without any fear of being ditched by God. This "anything goes" approach characterizing informal *dvaita* devotion is distinct from our typical relationships with people, where the fear of rejection so often lurks in the background. It is also in stark contrast with the more formal scripturally-based methods of worship in which specific rules must be adhered to, such as the *mantras* appropriate to various deities, the sequence of actions necessary to make the rituals successful and the required sacerdotal instruments.

So there are two distinct types of dualistic devotion. One is formal dualistic devotion prescribed in the scriptures in the form of specific devotional practices, as well as *karma yoga* and *upasana yoga*. The other is informal dualistic devotion as described in devotional literature in which one is free to interact with the Lord in any manner whatsoever. Neither of these dualistic practices is intended for liberation; rather both are meant for refining and purifying the mind. Formal dualistic devotion is compulsory for all freedom-seekers because it is specially designed for attaining the fourfold qualifications required for Vedantic inquiry.[5] By contrast, informal dualistic devotion is an optional add-on, optional because the practice of personifying God requires a particular, some might say peculiar, mindset unfamiliar to most Western seekers.

Informal dualistic devotion is distinct from the five compulsory acts of worship required by *karma yoga* known as the *pancha maha-yajnas*.[6] Informal dualistic devotion also has the benefit of refining emotionally turbulent minds, which is especially true for people who have difficult family

[5]These four qualifications, known as *sadhana chatushtaya sampatti*, are: (1) discrimination, (2) dispassion, (3) discipline – there are six inner disciplines: mind control, sense control, withdrawal, i.e. not being too extroverted, forbearance, faith in the Vedic scripture and freedom from distraction. One who has all four of these is called a qualified inquirer, or *adhikari*.

or interpersonal relationships. When our close relationships are unhealthy, we need healthy relationships to neutralize them. A human being without healthy relationships will be emotionally dysfunctional by definition. Emotionally disturbed people desperately look for companionship because the human mind requires good relationships for psychological health. Indeed psychologists talk considerably about the value of supportive relationships. Thus for the spiritual seeker whose mind is unsettled because of turbulent relationships, informal dualistic devotion is particularly useful. When an emotionally troubled person puts his or her head in the lap of a loving person – real or imagined – the pain is easier to bear. Children in joint families tend to be more emotionally healthy because there is always a supportive adult to depend on. Unfortunately, by and large joint families have been supplanted by nuclear families in which both parents work and are often stressed and self-absorbed when at home. Consequently modern children often have little emotional support. If a child does not develop emotional self-confidence, he will not individuate and will be unable to objectively evaluate his place in the world, thus condemning himself to endless emotional turmoil. A disturbed mind is incapable of listening to the liberation teachings, of reasoning effectively and of assimilating self-knowledge.

Formal dualistic devotion in the form of *karma yoga* and *upasana yoga*, with or without informal dualistic devotion, leads to self-inquiry, which leads to non-dual self-knowledge, otherwise known as non-dual devotion. Non-dual devotion is both freedom from the devotee and freedom for the devotee. If this progression is not clear when we study devotional literature, we risk getting trapped in the philosophy of devotion and getting permanently stalled. There are many useful devotional texts available, but we must consistently interpret them according to the traditional teachings of Vedanta if we want to obtain non-dual love. So although there are many written commentaries on the Narada devotion *sutras,* most conform to devotional philosophy rather than the Vedanta view.

[6]The five acts of worship, which are to be performed daily as a way of offsetting harm, expressing gratitude and purifying the mind, are: (1) *Deva Yajna,* homage to God and the elements, which includes meditation, (2) *Pitru Yajna,* homage to our parents and ancestors (e.g. taking good care of one's parents), (3) *Manushya Yajna,* homage to humanity (e.g. charity, social service, physical help or teaching – anything that one has to give), (4) *Bhuta Yajna,* homage to beings in the plant and animal kingdom (e.g. offering food and water), as well as preservation of the environment, (5) *Bramha Yagna* – worship of Vedic knowledge by studying the scriptures oneself and offering this knowledge to others.

Was Narada Enlightened?

The author of this text is Narada Maharshi, a great sage and well-known figure in Puranic literature. To determine whether Narada was a dualist or a non-dualist, in the seventh chapter of the *Chandogya Upanishad* we discover that he was a disciple of a great Vedanta teacher named Sanatkumara. In fact the chapter opens with Narada approaching Sanatkumara and making this beautiful statement:

> "I have indeed heard from teachers like you that a knower of self goes beyond this ocean of sorrow. I have no other resort except you, great master. Take me across this ocean of misery."

Narada has come to the conclusion that dualistic devotion leads to a pure mind, but not to *moksa* which will take care of his suffering. As a famous verse in Shankara's *Tattva Bodh* (38.3) says, "The knower of the self goes beyond all sorrows." The *Upanishads* tell us that the self is non-dual and that knowledge of it is required for liberation. So there is no doubt that Narada has non-dual devotion/knowledge. And although the explicit meaning of his words in these verses (*sutras*) may create an impression of duality, we come to non-dual devotion by extracting their implied meaning.

Study of dualistic devotional literature of both East and West reveals the fact that even great devotees suffer, sometimes immensely, because they retain the belief that they are separate from God, the object of their love. If you have any doubt on this point, read the diaries of Mother Teresa, who was recently canonized by the Catholic church. Had she had the benefit of Narada's *sutras*, the good *karma* to have heard the teaching of Vedanta and curiosity to inquire into Christ's most famous statement, "I and my Father are one," she may have been a suffering-free saint.

Free Will or Fate?

Sutras are cryptic, axiomatic nuggets of meaning on a particular topic that need to be unfolded in a particular way. Unlike the *Brahma Sutras,* a canonical Vedantic text (*jnana-grantha*) written in a rigid logical format, Narada's *sutras* on devotion is a comprehensive presentation and elucidation of the topic of devotion (*sutra grantha*).

Most of the commentaries on devotion present the idea that devotion is "total surrender." This idea – which seems to appeal to sincere but intellectually challenged individuals – involves a devotee simply giving himself or herself over to God by chanting the Lord's name until God swoops down from heaven and whisks him or her off to *moksa*. It is a reassuring message, but it is not in keeping with the teachings of Vedanta, which insists on the use of our free will. As the *Bhagavad Gita* (6.6) says, "One should uplift oneself by oneself. One should not lower oneself." Or pull God down to our level, Vedanta adds. We must not wash our hands of responsibility and put everything on God. To understand the deep and powerful message of this text then, we must interpret it in a manner consistent with the Vedantic view.

The Big Picture - a Roadmap

Every serious seeker of freedom needs to have a complete knowledge of the topic of devotion. Here are the steps: (1) informal dualistic devotion, (2) formal dualistic devotion, (3) self-inquiry, (4) non-dual devotion/knowledge and (5) liberation, or *moksa*. Informal dualistic devotion involves personifying God and relating to one's projection according to one's individual needs. It has many psychological benefits, and anyone attracted to it is encouraged to do so, but it is not considered a compulsory practice. Formal dualistic devotion, which is explained in the *Bhagavad Gita*, is *karma yoga* and *upasana yoga*. It is designed for developing the qualifications for liberation: discrimination, dispassion, discipline and burning desire for freedom. It is explained in several Vedantic texts, particularly the *Bhagavad Gita*. It is compulsory for Vedantic inquiry. As the *Bhagavad Gita* (4:3) says, "May you gain self-knowledge by prostration, service and proper inquiry. The wise sages will impart non-dual knowledge to you."

A "proper" inquirer is a qualified devotee, and a proper teacher is someone who has learned the wisdom of the *Vedas* and who belongs to the Vedantic lineage (*guru-shishya parampara*). A teacher who meets this qualification is said to be a *srotriya,* a person of right knowledge who can wield the means of knowledge skillfully. Secondly, the teacher must have fully assimilated non-dual self-knowledge and abide in the self as the self, which means that his love is unconditional. A teacher who meets this qualification is said to be a *brahmanishta,* established in limitlessness, meaning free of attachment to objects and satisfied with the self alone. Such a teacher will invariably introduce self-inquiry to the student at the appropriate time and lead him or her through the steps.

No Skipping

Non-dual devotion is non-dual knowledge, and non-dual knowledge is non-dual devotion. Dualistic devotion culminates in non-dual devotion, and non-dual devotion requires dualistic devotion in the form of *karma yoga* and *upasana yoga.* Choosing one or the other is not an option; they are sequential and mutually interdependent. Self-inquiry is the essential catalyst that converts dualistic devotion into non-dual devotion. Liberation (*moksa*), which is non-different from non-dual love, is the ultimate destination.

If we read devotional literature without clear awareness of this template, we risk getting ensnared by misconceptions and stunting or aborting our spiritual growth. The Narada devotion *sutras* is a beautiful text because it deals with the first four stages clearly and explicitly. Self-inquiry is not altogether absent from the text; rather it is implied. The implicit integration of Vedanta into the Narada devotion *sutras* is brought out in the following commentaries.

Words and Definitions

Subject and Object

When the text or the commentary speaks of objects, it is not speaking only of material objects, although one's love may be centered on material objects. Existence, the self, is non-dual but it appears as a conscious subject, whose nature is love, and as infinite inert objects. So an object is anything other than you, the ever-present conscious self. Your body, your feelings and your thoughts are objects. Your experiences are objects. In fact experience itself is an object. It is important to keep this definition in mind as you study these verses and commentaries if you wish to distinguish unconditional non-dual self-love from object-love. Knowing the difference between them is non-dual devotion.

Duality and Non-Duality

Duality, which is thought to be a fact, is the belief that the experienced separation of the subject from the object is an actual separation. Non-duality is the nature of existence. It means that, while duality seems to be real when reality is experienced through the senses, the subject and the objects are non-separate. Both are only consciousness, the self.

Samsara and *Samsaris*

Samsara is complete immersion in the belief that reality is a duality and that objects are necessary for happiness. It is characterized by suffering. It is brought on by ignorance of the non-dual nature of reality. A *samsari* is a worldly person, someone who thinks the subject and the objects are different and pursues objects for happiness.

Maya, Isvara, Bhagavan and God

Maya is the power in consciousness/awareness that creates objects and causes individuals to believe that reality is a duality. *Isvara* is a name for *Maya* favored by Vedantic inquirers. *Bhagavan* is a word for *Isvara/Maya* favored by devotees. *Isvara/Bhagavan* controls the behavior of objects with the law of *karma* and delivers the results of individual's actions to them. It is God.

Jiva

The word "*jiva*" means "the eternal individual," "the devotee" and "a specific individual," according to the context. It seems as if there are many unique individuals, but in fact there is only one human individual with assorted peculiarities. When Christ referred to himself as the "son" of God, he meant the eternal individual.

Self-Realized and Self-Actualized

Individuals are said to be self-realized when they understand that the experiencing subject and the objects of experience are non-separate. Individuals are self-actualized when their sense of doership disappears; they don't depend on objects for their happiness in any way, are perfectly satisfied with themselves as consciousness/awareness and are equally satisfied with themselves as created individuals. Self-realization is brought about by self-knowledge (Vedanta), and self-actualization is accomplished by the application of self-knowledge to one's life. Self-realized individuals know they are free, but enjoy varying degrees of attachment to objects; self-actualized individuals are free, i.e. completely non-attached to objects. If a self-realized person is qualified when self-knowledge dawns, he or she immediately becomes self-actualized.

Me and I

Many of the quotations from the *Bhagavad Gita* appear in the first person because the text personifies God as a fully actualized person.

He

I mainly use the pronoun "he" instead of "he/she" to avoid clumsy sentences. *Isvara* and *jiva,* the devotee, have no gender.

Chapter I

The Nature of the Highest Devotion

The Enlightened Person

THE VERSES BEGIN with the topic of non-dual devotion and later introduce dualistic devotion, the stepping stone to non-duality, as does the *Bhagavad Gita,* which introduces self-knowledge first, followed by *karma yoga* and *upasana yoga*. This chapter presents a picture of a fully self-actualized person, an embodiment of non-dual love.

1. "Now, therefore, we shall teach the logic of devotion."

People become devoted to God for logical reasons and evolve in a logical sequence. The following verse from the *Bhagavad Gita* (7:16) says, "Four types of virtuous people surrender to me (*Isvara*): the distressed (*artha*), wealth- and pleasure-seekers (*artharthi*), seekers of self-knowledge (*jignasu*) and the wise (*jnani*)." The first three are dualistic devotees with various motives, the last is a fully self-actualized person.

The distressed devotee is emotionally dysfunctional and wants relief: "Fix me, Lord! I am so miserable." The security-oriented devotee wants worldly objects: security, pleasure, position, recognition, children, employment – any blessed thing. The seeker of knowledge is more spiritually evolved and asks the Lord for (1) the qualifications necessary to understand the truth of reality, (2) a proper teacher of self-inquiry and, ultimately, (3) self-knowledge.

Have Your Cake and Eat It Too

The *jnani* devotee, or wise person, is a non-dual devotee. Lest one imagine that devotion and non-duality are mutually exclusive, Vedanta informs us that since non-dual reality enjoys two orders, the real (*satya*) and the apparently real (*mithya*), which are not in conflict, the *jnani's* personality can worship the Lord in the form of objects and experiences, while the *jnani,* who is the self, simultaneously enjoys the ever-present, ever-experienced, non-dual love that is the nature of the self.

Unfortunately, anti-intellectualism is rife in the modern spiritual world and many teachers and teachings mislead people with the idea that the path of inquiry is only one of many possible paths for attaining liberation (all roads lead to Rome!). Unfortunately, only one road – self-knowledge – leads to *moksa* because the inquirer/devotee is already free and non-dual love is his nature; he simply doesn't understand this fact. Furthermore, the uninformed say that Vedanta is a challenging, dry, intellectual path that smart people avoid since dualistic devotion is suitable – read: pleasant and easy – for these trying materialistic times because the devotee gains wonderful experiences that are not available for dry intellectuals. At the same time, they ignore the inconvenient truth that the juicy and varied mystic experiences they lustfully covet inevitably end, plunging the devotee into predictable emotional frustrations and depressions. The experiential view of enlightenment is anti-Vedic. It is not taught in the *Bhagavad Gita,* in which the teacher, speaking as *Isvara,* says:

> "Among the four types, the distressed, the seeker of wealth, the seeker of knowledge and the wise, the wise person is superior because he is ***continually and exclusively*** engaged in devotional service. I am extremely dear to that cultivator of wisdom and he is likewise dear to me." (7:17)

The words "continually and exclusively" mean that the experience of non-dual love brought on by self-inquiry does not come and go as do mystical experiences – *satoris, samadhis* and epiphanies of all ilk. Whereas experience requires constant effort, knowledge is effortless. "Devotional service" does not refer to specific devotional practices but to a mind/heart that is continually and effortlessly aware that its nature is love.

There is nothing wrong with approaching God when you are distressed or desirous of objects, but if you understand that the pursuit of all objects is actually a pursuit of *moksa* because you gain freedom (momentarily) when you get what you want, you will be forced to conclude that you should convert your desire for objects into a desire to know who you are since the self is ever-free. Momentary freedom/happiness should not be scoffed at, but it plays second fiddle to permanent freedom and non-dual love.

2. "Non-dual devotion (*advaita bhakti*) is supreme love of 'this.'"

Non-dual devotion is love of God with extreme ("supreme") attachment because it is based on the fact that God is ever-present unconditional love and that the alternative, love of objects – the "not-self" – is conditional and inherently unsatisfying.

Does the verse refer to a specific God or does it refer to the self, limitless consciousness? This is a legitimate question because the *karmic* section of the *Vedas* – and all world religions – presents God as an extraordinary divine being who is the object of worship and meditation. Is this God who is worthy of the non-dual devotee's complete attention the all-pervasive self or is it a specific deity? It is limitless, ever-present consciousness/existence, the one observer of all objects and the knower of all gods, not a discrete personified deity:

> "This self cannot be seen, but it sees. It cannot be heard, but it hears. It cannot be thought of, but it thinks. It cannot be understood, but it understands. There is no seer other than the self. There is no hearer other than that. There is no thinker other than that." (*Brihadaranyaka Upanishad,* 3.7.23)

> "It is the Ear of the ear, the Mind of the mind, the Speech of speech, the Life of life, and the Eye of the eye. After giving up identification with the senses and renouncing this world, inquiring men become immortal." (*Kena Upanishad,* 1:1-2)

If there is more than one God, then each God must have a self, which means that there are many selves. In fact religious people believe in a multiplicity of individuals and a multiplicity of special gods because they speak of "my God" and "your God," invariably implying that "my" God is superior to "your" God. However, Vedanta points out the fact that there is only one God, the self – existence/consciousness/love – that lives in the heart of all gods. Better yet, Vedanta says that there is only God:

> "The Lord lives in the heart of all beings. By its power to delude it causes them to dance as if they were puppets on a string." (*Bhagavad Gita,* 18:61)

And Krishna, the teacher, speaking as the self, makes it clear the God, "this," is ever-present, all-pervasive, eternal consciousness/awareness when he talks about the various forms of the Lord in the creation:

> "I am the self that resides in the heart of all beings. I am the beginning, the middle and the end of all beings." (10:20)

This God Is Always Present and Available

Obviously, if you are the beginning, middle and end of anything, you are something beyond beginnings, middles and ends. You are timeless, i.e. eternal. Because there is only one existence, there is only one eternity, a temporal metaphor indicating the self. This is an important verse because it refers to God as "this" (*aparoksha*). Dualists see God as a Someone Else who lives Elsewhere. For them God is always a far-away "that" ensconced in some unavailable heaven or floating in some mystical and mysterious transcendental sky. But Vedanta says that the distance between you and God is zero. It is your innermost self, your essence, that without which you are not you.

So non-dual devotion is complete, unconditional, "supreme" love of yourself. Dualists are victims of *Maya's* power to reverse (*viparaya*) the relationship between the subject – the ever-present self – and the objects that present themselves to it – the "not-self." For them the reflected self, the individual, is the only self and God is an object of this individual's love. So they believe that self-love is hubris, the work of the "Devil," i.e. ignorance. In fact worship of something other than you is ignorance because there is no one other than you. When you identify with the person you have been conditioned to think you are, God can only be an object.

You Never Love Anyone Else

However, the *Upanishads,* particularly the *Brihadaranyaka Upanishad,* tells us that for every human being – instinctively, universally and unconditionally – the highest love is self-love. Vedanta accepts the existence of an individual reflected self, a soul, but encourages worship of the non-separate "innermost" self. As it says in the *Brihadaranyaka Upanishad* (1.4.8):

> "This innermost self is dearer than a son, dearer than wealth, dearer than everything else. A person who knows the self to be the dearest is certainly justified when he says those who think anyone or anything else is dearer than they are. Whatever object you love will die one day. You should meditate on the limitless self alone. The dear ones you love are not immortal."

People and things can be dear and dearer. They can even be undear. But they are never the dearest.

But what about my spouse and children? Yajnavalkya addresses this doubt very clearly in the following verse from the *Brihadaranyaka Upanishad* (2.4.5):

> "It is not for the sake of the husband that the husband is loved, but for the sake of the self. It is not for the sake of the wife that the wife is loved, but for the sake of the self. It is not for the sake of children that children are loved, but for the sake of the self. It is not for the sake of wealth that wealth (or pleasure or virtue) is loved, but for the sake of the self. It is not for the sake of the world that the world is loved, but for the sake of the self. Everything is loved only for the self's sake. Consequently this self should be realized. Listen to the teachings about it, reflect on what you have heard and meditate diligently on it. By realizing the self through these means, everything is known."

An Inconvenient - but Liberating - Truth

Although reality is non-dual, owing to the power of *Maya* it seems to be a duality. To those ignorant of the nature of reality, there are "others." When *Maya* is operating, the love that I am is experientially unavailable, so I love what I see, usually human beings or animals, even material objects. I love "others," not knowing that they are apparent others, not real others. I love myself 24/7 unconditionally and I love everything other than me conditionally, the condition being my happiness. Why do I want to be happy all the time? Because I love myself always. If you make me happy, i.e. if you do what I want or conform to my idea of what I want, I may love you. But the moment you become an impediment to my happiness, my love starts to dry up. I may continue to care for you out of obligation, but as long as you don't contribute to my comfort I cannot love you. This may be a difficult fact to face but it proves one incontrovertible truth: the highest love is reserved for oneself alone. There are no exceptions to this rule.

Therefore the "God" to which Narada is referring is none other than the self. Love with total attachment is called non-dual devotion. Total attachment means that there is no other option. It is synonymous with self-love. We instinctively and naturally love the self alone.

Self-realization, or self-knowledge, sometimes called enlightenment, is the hard and fast knowledge "I am limitless consciousness and not the body/mind/sense complex" brought about by exposing the mind to the teachings of Vedanta. Those who do not understand that self-knowledge and love are one often criticize Vedanta as a "merely intellectual" path, implying that the path of love is superior because it produces states of ecstatic love.

No Unique Path of Love

Since Swami Vivekananda presented his lectures on Yoga around the turn of the twentieth century, generations of Indian and Western seekers have been under the spell of the multi-path confusion, which presents devotional *yoga* as a path unique to the predominant psychology of the individual.

According to Vivekananda, in addition to physical (*hatha*) *yoga* there are four paths to liberation: *bhakti yoga, karma yoga, jnana yoga* and *raja,* or *ashtanga, yoga.* The path of devotion (*bhakti*) is meant to serve the needs of predominately emotional persons. The path of action (*karma*) is only suitable for extroverted, action-oriented people, and the path of knowledge (*jnana*) is designed for those with an intellectual orientation. And *raja yoga,* the eightfold (*ashtanga*) path, is for anyone who is not one of first three.

Oddly, Vivekananda seems oblivious to the fact that you can only get what you already have – freedom – by understanding that you are free now and have always been free. Furthermore, he seems not to know that knowledge requires a means, and action is not a valid means of knowledge. And finally, every seeker has a physical body, emotional and intellectual centers, so practicing only one path would seriously limit the harmonious integration of the psyche. So, ironically, even though he was considered an enlightened soul and a champion of the *Vedas* and the Vedic way of life, his ideas about love and Vedanta are, if not anti-Vedic, certainly quasi-Vedic.

If someone thinks of himself as a devotee exclusively, this identity is not warranted, because devotional practices like *pujas,* chanting and meditation/prayer, are all *karmas,* activities. So in fact this person is a *karma yogi,* a doer of ritualistic actions. Additionally, devotion is not a quality unique to any individual or path, but is found in anyone pursuing a spiritual or worldly goal. One does not pursue self-knowledge or self-experience without devotion, for example. So the idea of devotion as a particular path is not found in the *Vedas,* although the topic of devotion is central to them.

Furthermore, we need to mention that Vedanta is the knowledge behind all paths, so it could not be said to be a path at all. Since the distance between you and your self is exactly zero, how will you get there? However, leaving these arguments aside, Vedanta might reasonably be called a "pathless path," as it encourages action and action always leads somewhere. Insofar as it is a path, we contend that it is a path of love that leads to the realization that the self is love. It is a path of action that leads to the realization the self is love and it is a path of knowledge that leads to the hard and fast understanding "I am love itself."

The Connection between Love and Consciousness

Most seekers are unable to connect the idea of the self as consciousness/awareness and the self as love. There is a logical connection: if reality is non-dual consciousness as Vedanta contends and if love exists - which it does - then there can be no difference between love and consciousness.

This argument convinces few because basically nobody sees reality as a non-duality, so we need to reveal a simple, practical connection between love and consciousness. The bridge between them is attention. In terms of the apparent reality, love is attention. To say that I love my cat means that I pay attention to it. I feed it, cuddle it and think about it. If I do not pay attention to my husband or wife, he or she will inform me that I do not love him or her and will probably file for divorce. Attention is consciousness directed through the Heart (the Subtle Body) toward an object. The fact that I am always paying attention to something means that I am always loving something. This is a very difficult fact to grasp because we are conditioned to believe that love is a special state or a special feeling. But it isn't. It is the nature of consciousness, my self (*anandam*). It does not come from objects, though certain objects invoke it.

So What About Hate?

You may argue that there are many things that you do not love, but this is true only because it pleases you not to love a particular object. It pleases you not to love an object, because you love your dislikes even though you are always free not to dislike something; nobody has a gun to your head with reference to where your attention goes. Not loving an object because you dislike the object does not mean that your nature is not love. It means that for the sake of yourself, which you love above all objects, you indulge a dislike. Your likes and dislikes, fears and desires, do not come from outside. They bubble up from within you. They are born of consciousness, your awareness, which is love and which is free of them as it is filtered by ignorance.

Likes are "positive" love, and dislikes are "negative" love. They are you, but you – love – are free of them. As soon as you realize how silly they are, you won't feed them and they will disappear.

If you say that you do not like your job but remain in it because you need the money, it only means that you love money more than you dislike the job. And you love money because you love yourself; you think that the things money can buy can make you happy and – to repeat – you want yourself to be happy because you love you. Everything we do, everything we think and feel is for the sake of the self. It is difficult to accept the fact that you do not love an object for the sake of the object, because we want to believe that we love unselfishly. But all love is self-"ish" because there is only one self. The object that you love or don't love is just you, appearing as the idea of an "other" in your consciousness.

Love is the natural attraction of the mind toward objects which it believes are a source of happiness. I "love" chocolate because it gives me happiness. In the case of material objects, we generally use the word "like," whereas in the case of living beings we use the word "love," but there is no difference.

There is nothing "wrong" with loving objects, particularly if the love is informed with the knowledge that all objects are the self. But love of objects without self-knowledge is defective. Love of objects is not eternal, decaying as one's attraction to the object wanes. It is also prone to turn to its opposite, duality being what it is. People may initially love each other and decide to get married to get to know each other more intimately, but often after some time they say, "I loved you once, but now I would love you to go away." In the beginning we only notice compatibilities, but as time passes incompatibilities peek through and puncture the love bubble, whereupon my darling bundle of joy quickly becomes a darling bundle of misery, even though he/she has not actually changed.

Love Is Attraction to an Object that Is a Source of Joy

Therefore the definition of love is "***mental attraction toward an object that is a source of joy.***" Attraction to objects is relationship-love. Attraction to one's self is non-dual love.

Duality is the belief that the conscious subject and the object of its affections are different. To state the obvious, relationship-love is dualistic love. It is a very wonderful thing until you realize, almost immediately, that it is fraught with anxiety. When you are caught in duality, even though the love that you are is fullness itself, you believe that you lack love. Ignorance of this fact causes you to project love onto objects. It makes you think that if you possessed a relationship with a particular object – let's say a person – you would feel complete. The feeling of completeness is the experience of love, your self. The knowledge of your completeness is liberation. It results in an acute appreciation of the fact that "I am love."

I Don't Love You, I Love Love

If you love love, you love the self because the self is love. Passion for an object, particularly a person, is not love, even though desire is a form of love. But if you look into it you will discover that when you love someone or something, it is your self – the love – in the object that you love. You do not know that when you contact the object you are only contacting yourself. The object invokes the love that you are. The joy is never in the object. Because of ignorance of this fact, you become attached to the idea that you need the object, usually a living being of some sort, to complete you. This kind of "love" is thought to be love, but it is ignorance masquerading as love.

The desire to love an object and be loved by an object is the primary cause of suffering because it generates an incessant stream of binding emotions, both positive and negative. Nonetheless, it is not a desire that can be immediately renounced, as it is hardwired from birth. So it needs to be sublimated, not by demanding and expecting love, but by giving it. Giving love is the essence of devotion. It is the simple recognition that by your very presence as consciousness you are offering yourself to the world in the form of your thoughts, words and deeds. It is awareness of the presence of "others" and their need for love. You do not lose love by loving, because love is infinite. On the contrary, your experience of yourself as love grows the more you give. Devotional *yoga* is also loving the "you" you think you are – the poor dear that wants love – because from the point of view of the self, the actual lover, that "you" is an object too. It redeems the loveless past.

Because every transaction with an object is actually love, owing to the fact that the self is love and there is nothing but the self, how do we account for fear and pain? If the doer, the cognitive person, is ignorant of her nature as love, the love will be hijacked by his or her likes and dislikes and expressed in negative, often perverted, ways. Electricity flowing through a radio manifests as sound, through a lamp as light. Consciousness/love flowing through a dislike manifests as a nasty word, and through a like as a kind word.

Inquiry aids devotion because it makes the cognitive person, the Subtle Body, aware of its prejudices and biases, likes and dislikes. When you are aware of your projections, they subside and the energy invested in them is converted into devotion; you love yourself more because you have freed yourself of painful emotions.

You Have No Option

If you accept these facts and this definition of love, there is no option but to unconditionally love the self – **because it is the only causeless and abiding source of happiness.** As it says in the *Chandogya Upanishad* (7.23.1), "The infinite alone is bliss, which is not present in finite objects," objects that seem to be a source of joy and only reflect your innate love.

So love of "this" (God) is self-love. The word "God" (*Isvara*) may give students of Vedanta cause for doubt because God is pure original consciousness **plus *Maya*.** Pure original consciousness does not create the world of objects. So is Narada saying that love of God is love of the Creator or love of the uncreated self? The question is moot because there is no difference between the pure original consciousness and pure original consciousness associated with *Maya*. *Maya* produces the ignorance and the objects, but since we know that love of objects results in sorrow and Vedanta's sole reason for being is removal of sorrow, Narada can only mean love of pure original consciousness.

Additionally, since pure original consciousness includes God and the creation, love of self includes love of objects. Before non-dual devotion takes place, the inquirer thinks he is a unique *jiva,* and should love the Creator to obtain the qualifications since the pure original self does not see *jivas,* qualified or unqualified. But once the qualifications are in place and the knowledge takes place, the creation is known to be *mithya,* as good as non-existent, since the objects are known to be unreal and there is no place for the love to go but to the self.

> "Experiencing one's own self in all beings and all beings in the self, one attains [the status of] limitless awareness and not by any other means." (*Kaivalya Upanishad*, verse 10)

Likewise, the *Bhagavad Gita* (6:29-30) says:

> "One whose mind is disciplined through inquiry perceives the self in all beings and all beings in the self. All objects are valued equally by him. I [the self] am not lost to the one

> who sees me everywhere and sees everything in me. And he is not lost to me."

This love is called non-dual devotion because God, the self, and every living being are one. Non-dual devotion alone is real love. It is the highest form of devotion.

3. "The nectar of immortality is the essence of non-dual love."

One of the world's most famous devotees, Jesus Christ, said, "On this rock I build my church," which I interpret as, "On the ever-present, unchanging self I construct my holy life." Only universal, unconditional, immortal love is perfect security, the number-one human value. Conditional love is – well – conditional.

> "So long as a man is fit and able to support his family, see the affection the family shows him. But they no longer care to have a word with him when his body totters due to old age. Seek the self." (Shankaracharya, *Bhaja Govindam*)

You will be loved by others only as long as you are pleasing and useful or at least until they are sure you have written them into your will. But if you become a liability, they quickly pack you off to the old folks home. Don't expect too much from the world or you will suffer. Seek the self. Seek real love.

Non-Duality - What's in It For Me?

The benefits of non-dual devotion are elaborately discussed in the *Bhagavad Gita*.

The text does not describe the non-dual devotee's behavior, but speaks of his or her state of mind. It says these devotees are always satisfied in themselves and do not depend on others for their happiness. They are free of attachment, hatred, desire, anger, fear, elation, depression, etc. They are friendly, compassionate, equanimous, forbearing, contented, self-controlled, devoted, gentle, pure, resourceful and impartial.

To complete the picture, a negative definition is offered. The non-dual devotee, otherwise described as a "wise person," is free of hatred, a sense of uniqueness, specialness, entitlement and ownership. He or she is not subject to anxiety, elation, envy, fear, dependence, selfish action, grief, desire and the pairs of opposites, e.g. pleasure/pain, praise/censure, etc.

These people are not subject to anxiety, because being already satisfied in the self as the self, they do not initiate actions and wait for the results to make them feel whole and complete. They are fearless because they don't see duality. Fear is born of duality. They don't get elated when positive things enter their *karma* streams, because they are elated by the bliss of their true natures. They don't depend on objects for happiness, because they are completely happy in themselves. They are not selfish, because there is nothing to gain by obtaining or hanging onto objects. They are generous because they enjoy making people happy. Although they enjoy objects, they don't suffer grief when objects decay and disappear, because they are non-attached to them, gladly accepting the obvious fact that anything that comes eventually goes. And they are not fascinated by *samsara,* where the pairs of opposites rule, because they understand that *samsara* is a zero-sum game: the upside of everything is balanced by the downside. There is no winning or losing.

Is an Enlightened Person a Saint?

Is this non-dual devotee a saint? Many people in the spiritual world can't accept Vedanta's idea of enlightenment, because they confuse enlightenment with sainthood. They imagine that enlightened people are in some kind of superhuman "state" where no objects are experienced and there is no experiencing entity to experience normal human emotions, except – inexplicably – endless bliss, which they are meant to shower on the world. Or they imagine that self-realization will transform the *jiva* into a saint. Insufficiency and inadequacy alone account for magical thinking. Self-realized people may be saintlike, but they are not saints, totally pure *jivas.* In fact saints are not totally pure *jivas.* A *jiva,* an individual, is always a mixture of positive and negative characteristics because *jivas* exist in duality. The self is totally pure, but it is not a *jiva.* You only "gain" purity by understanding that you are the self. You cannot "become" pure.

Reality is one non-dual awareness/existence that, owing to the power of *Maya,* appears as a duality, an apparently discrete subject and a variety of objects. The verse means that "the devotee" knows he or she is non-dual love and that the thoughts and emotions that he or she experiences – positive or negative – are not real (*mithya*), so there is no identification with them. When consciousness – you – identify with a thought or feeling, a like or dislike, the feeling seems to be real. The more you dwell on it, the more substantial it becomes. The feeling seems like "the truth" because you, the truth, are associating with it. But it is not the truth. It is just a mechanical material tendency generated by the *jiva's karma* stream.

Having said that, while negative emotions born of self-ignorance may continue to manifest initially after self-knowledge takes place, they eventually disappear for want of reinforcement. This does not create positive qualities – discrimination, dispassion, compassion and the like – because they are already present in the *Isvara* part of you, the unconscious mind. They are simply unobstructed, so they manifest in you. Your *jiva* is *Isvara's* instrument. So if non-dual compassion is expressed, it is *Isvara* expressing, not the devotee's *jiva*. In the unenlightened, compassion is, however, obscured by ignorance-born tendencies. So for a *jiva* to become a saint, he or she will have to act like his or her idea of a pure person, which, if you have the slightest familiarity with the modern spiritual scene, is enough to turn your stomach.

These characteristics or benefits of liberation, including the immortality and perfection benefit discussed in the *Gita,* form the basis for the following *sutras.*

4. "One who obtains non-dual devotion becomes perfect, immortal and fully satisfied.

Most of us would like to be perfect. We strive for perfect circumstances, jobs, bodies, children, lovers and security. The "supermom" is a worldly person who strives to do motherhood perfectly. Spiritually inclined types are often bedeviled by a sense of spiritual and moral inferiority: "I am too selfish, greedy, controlling and dishonest. I want to be pure, holy and saintly, like Christ or Mother Teresa." Consequently they subject themselves to various self-abnegating disciplines and "selfless" activities that they feel will make them less imperfect and more perfect. However lovely it makes you feel that you are becoming a better person and no matter how useful it is to obtain the kind of mind that is suitable for inquiry, striving for *jiva*-perfection is subject to one glaring contradiction: no matter how hard you try to become perfect and no matter how much progress you make toward the realization of your goal, you will never reach perfection, because every step forward causes the goal to recede by one step; at every level you become aware of new imperfections that need to be removed; such is the nature of *samsara*! This is so because the notion that you are imperfect is not true. Additionally, the idea that you are a devotee and that what you seek – non-dual love – is different from you is also not true. No one will ever become perfect by doing anything. Imperfection is the nature of *samsara.* Imagine a perfect circle saying, "I want to become more round."

Exercise Your Free Will

Narada says that you will become perfect if you obtain non-dual devotion. Yet how can you "obtain" non-dual devotion – which is freedom from and freedom for the devotee – by action, since action is caused by a limited doer and perfection is limitlessness? All you can do to become perfect is to prepare your mind with *karma yoga* and *upasana yoga* until *Isvara* creates the circumstances – the scripture and a qualified teacher – that allow you to diligently expose your mind to Vedanta. When you do, you will discover the idea that you are imperfect was based on the erroneous belief that you, the eternal *Jiva,* which is non-separate from perfect, ever-present and always-available non-dual consciousness, are merely an individual *jiva,* i.e. the body/mind/sense complex, is not true. To read this verse without understanding the implied process of self-realization – the roadmap to non-dual devotion – may cause you to think that devotional *yoga* has some special technique that will produce a powerful experience of non-dual love that will transform the limited *jiva* into a perfect being.

Vedanta makes it abundantly clear that the conversion of dualistic devotion into non-dual devotion doesn't happen automatically and that nobody else can do it for us. Self-inquiry in the form of hearing, reasoning and assimilating under the guidance of a proper *guru* is the only bridge connecting dualistic devotion to non-dual devotion. For example, the *Bhagavad Gita* (4.34) says:

> "May you gain knowledge by prostration, service and proper inquiry. The wise sages will impart that knowledge to you."
>
> And, "To understand Reality one must humbly approach a proper teacher who is learned in the *Vedas* and, having made that knowledge his own, revel in it." (*Mundaka Upanishad,* 1.2.12)

There is no mention of this process in devotional literature, because devotees think that love is a special path that is completely disconnected from self-knowledge. A person who successfully goes through these stages will no longer find themselves caught in the seeking struggle, which has anxiety built into it. Seekers are always bedeviled by the thought, "When will I reach my destination?" which puts tremendous pressure on the devotee to prematurely claim enlightenment. The struggle ends with the realization that the devotee's nature is the fullness of love. In India there is a kind of unleavened deep-fried bread called *puri*. When a ball of *puri* batter is dropped in hot oil, it inflates like a balloon. As it expands, it moves around in the oil because it is not yet full. But once it has become full, it comes to rest. Similarly, we run about in the burning cauldron of *samsara* until we realize our completeness.

To say that I am full and complete non-dual consciousness is to say that I am immortal. *Samsaris* are caught in the clutches of time. Because they identify with their equipment, at every turn of *samsara's* restless wheel they believe that they are mortal and decaying. It is obvious that *Jiva's* equipment will never become immortal. I once met an Ayurvedic person who had spent thirty years in India seeking an Immortal to teach him *kayakalpa,* the method by which one can supposedly make the body immortal. When I suggested that if it worked there would be immortals on every street corner, he got up and walked away. Neither the body nor the mind can be made immortal. So the "becoming" of which Narada speaks is an understanding brought about by contemplation of the teaching "I am everything that is. I am Existence itself. I am pure, ever-full, non-dual love (*anandam*)." The cry of every human heart is expressed in this verse from the *Brihadaranyaka Upanishad*:

> "Lead me from the apparently real to the real, from the darkness of ignorance to the light of self-knowledge, from death – a sense of limitation – to immortality [fullness, limitlessness, liberation]."

Only non-dual devotion is absolute satisfaction.

> "Satisfied with oneself in oneself as oneself, when one no longer identifies with desires obtaining in the mind, one is said to be of firm knowledge and wise." (*Bhagavad Gita,* 2.55)

> And, "If there is a person who loves the self alone, who is happy with the self alone and who is contented with the self alone, this person has nothing left to accomplish." (3.17)

5. "One who attains it becomes completely desireless, grieves not, hates not and does not rejoice in life's fleeting happinesses. These people are no longer *jiva*-centered and are free of passion for objects."

A non-dual devotee is free of desires because he understands that they are born out of a sense of incompleteness, a lack of fullness. A man who wants to marry is trying to convert his bachelor self into a husband self for the sake of a feeling of completeness. When the feeling of completeness starts to feel incomplete he wants to convert that husband self into a father self, and when the father self begins to feel incomplete he needs to convert the father to a father-in-law self. It goes on and on. Even on one's deathbed one does not feel full. Non-dual devotion arises with the knowledge "I am fullness itself." This fullness is a permanent feeling of satisfaction and confidence, not an emotion.

> "All experiences enter the mind of a wise person through the senses, but they create no agitation, because he is full in himself, just as rivers pouring into the ocean do not disturb it. Because he is full, he is not a seeker of experiences." (*Bhagavad Gita,* 2.70)

When you ask for something, you may not get it, but when you discover the fullness that is your nature, even though you don't want or need anything, every experience is a pleasure. If the non-dual devotee desires at all, the desires are born of fullness; they are not tainted by self-interest and they only bless the world. Although they have nothing left to accomplish for themselves, they tirelessly act for the well-being of the world.

Happy to Be Reborn

Non-dual devotees are free of hatred. The greatest human being I ever met was a *swami* from Kerala, South India: Swami Abhedananda. In fact it would not be a stretch to say that he was God in human form. Of course we are all God in human form, but his human form, as far as I could see, was as free of duality as is humanly possible. When he was about to die one of his devotees asked if he wanted to be reborn. Naturally, *samsaris* don't want to be reborn, because they dislike the world insofar as they see it as a veil of tears. But the Swami said yes, much to the devotee's surprise. So she asked why. "So I can sing the praises of the Lord," he said without a trace of irony.

Non-dual self-actualized devotees have no desire to escape the world. In fact in that world I met many who were amused by seekers who were attempting to escape the world. One said to me, "What is there to escape from? Everything is the Lord. If you do manage to escape, you will only escape into the arms of the Lord."

Non-dual devotees do not grieve. From the perspective of the *jiva* the momentum of their previous actions continues to produce pleasant and unpleasant situations, but they are not bothered when *jiva*-conducive circumstances turn into unconducive experiences. Nor does pleasure create attachment for them, because they understand full well the zero-sum nature of the apparent reality. It should be obvious, but pleasure-seekers, blinded by desire, seem to forget that anything that begins ends. They revel in objects – security and pleasure – vainly.

But neither do the wise avoid sense pleasures; they simply do not get excited and make a big story about them. Comparing non-dual devotees with *samsaris* with reference to pleasure, Swami Paramarthananda says, "Their attitude is one of controlled enjoyment. It is like the difference between rash driving and fast driving. Fast drivers control speed. If a child were to run across the road, this driver would be able to brake in time. Rash drivers are accident-prone because the excitement of speed controls them. The wise person's enjoyment of sense pleasures is like fast driving, whereas the ignorant person's enjoyment of pleasure involves risk."

Samsaris are basically only interested in themselves. Because they need others, they pretend to serve them, but their service is not genuine. They believe that the world is solely intended to make them happy. They do not see that the world only works when everyone makes their contribution. Non-dual devotees see no difference between themselves and everyone else, so their actions are not tinged with selfishness.

6. "When non-dual devotion is attained, one is wonderstruck, immersed in silence and intoxicated with the self."

A "spiritual" person takes seriously the "what am I doing here on earth?" question that occurs regularly in every human mind. He is looking for "meaning" in the face of *samsara's* obvious pointlessness and sincerely seeks liberation. We know that liberation is the purpose of human life because every action people do is an attempt to remove a nagging sense of limitation. And while liberation is liberation from experience, insofar as it reveals the seeker's true identity, non-dual awareness/bliss, to be free of experience the *jiva* remains as an experiencing entity. Having discovered the non-difference of *Jiva* and *Isvara,* the person and its environment, the liberated non-dual devotee is thrilled – wonderstruck – that he has fulfilled his purpose in life. The more he thinks about how rare it is, the more intoxicated he becomes. Unlike the joy of winning the lottery, which eventually loses its allure, the joy of non-dual self-actualization grows and grows.

> "The following blessings, obtained only by the grace of God are rare and difficult to achieve: a human birth, the desire for liberation and association with a great sage." (Shankaracharya)

Innumerable species are born in the universe, so being born a human being is very rare. And even after gaining a human birth, countless are the goals one is tempted to pursue. Exceptionally rare are those who choose freedom as their primary goal. And even after discovering that freedom is possible, one enters the thicket of spirituality where dozens of systems prescribe a plethora of methods for attaining freedom. Which one to choose? So when the non-dual devotee reflects on the innumerable dead ends that have been avoided, he is thrilled to have been brought by *Isvara* to Vedanta.

As Vidyaranya says in the seventh chapter of *Panchadasi*:

> "Oh, how grand and true are the scriptures! How great and grand is my teacher and how amazing is my good fortune! Oh, wonderful is this bliss, this bliss!"

All spiritual teachings except Vedanta try to provide some kind of special experience here in this world as an antidote to the many problematic experiences visited on us, because they believe in the duality of subject and object, even as they claim that reality is non-dual. Just as inquirers we exhausted our patience with the "real" world, we eventually become exhausted trying to escape it, because all offered escapes are just worldly distractions. And just as we are about to throw in the towel, Vedanta comes along and tells us that there is no experiential solution, because the tangible world of experience is not real. What use are your spiritual experiences if experience itself is not real?

Who is prepared to believe it? Out of pure limitless consciousness *Maya* manufactures an exciting and variegated world of objects. In fact after years of inquiry many are still unable to assimilate the knowledge that the world is unreal. At the same time, we are informed that the self – which nobody ever saw, can see now or will ever see in the future – is the only reality. What a wonder! And then too, Vedanta challenges us to dismiss this statement: the self alone is real, the world is seemingly real. We cannot dismiss it, because all our knowledge is gained by perception and by inferences based on perception. And to top it off, it confidently proves a statement that seekers want to believe but cannot believe, because it is so counter-intuitive: "I am unborn, limitless impersonal consciousness and the only source of joy." How can it be true when I experience so many emotional problems, financial problems, love problems, knowledge problems, etc? Some days it is virtually impossible just to smile. What a wonder!

> "Some see the self as a wonder. Others speak of it as a wonder. Another hears that it is wonderful. Still, in spite of hearing of it, nobody seems to understand it at all." (*Bhagavad Gita,* 2:29)

And the *Katha Upanishad* (1.2.7):

> "Many do not even hear of it. Many who have heard of it cannot comprehend it. It is rare to find a good teacher and equally rare to find a qualified inquirer. Wonderful indeed is the one who comprehends it when taught by an able preceptor."

And in the *Taittiriya Upanishad* (part 3, *Bhriguvalli,* verse 10), Sage Bhrigu sings:

> "Bliss! Bliss! Bliss! I am food and I am the eater of food. I am the one that brings the food and the eater together. I am the firstborn of the true, the eternal and immortal. I am the immortal center, prior to the gods. Whoever hands down this knowledge preserves it. I am luminous like the sun. He who knows this attains the aforementioned results."

What a great wonder! I am the non-dual reality and I myself also appear as the experiencing *jiva,* the experienced universe and the experience connecting it all together. By the amazing power of *Maya,* I play as the world, the *jiva* and *Isvara,* the Creator. The seven wonders of the world pale to insignificance in the face of this amazing knowledge!

What Happened to *Isvara*?

Narada makes an interesting and seemingly paradoxical statement: the non-dual devotee "revels in himself." First he defined devotion as supreme love of God and now devotion is "intoxication" or enjoyment of one's self. This statement can only be true if God is non-different from the self. Plus or minus *Maya,* pure awareness is still pure, limitless, non-dual, ever-present, whole and complete awareness. Nowhere in the devotional *darshana* will you find such a statement, because it obliterates the distinction between the devotee and God. To arrive at this understanding we need to accept the teachings of Vedanta, appreciate the unexamined logic that proves the identity of *Isvara* and *Jiva* and check with our own experience to see if it isn't true. As Krishna says (*Bhagavad Gita,* 10.20), "I am the self residing in the heart of all beings."

7. "It does not generate desires, as by its nature it inclines one to renunciation of objects."

If you are full, you are the meaning of your life. If you are the meaning, what use is there for objects? They don't validate you, you validate them. Objects, for the non-dual devotee, are purely utilitarian; they cannot add to the fullness he experiences. This devotee is like Teflon: nothing sticks to him.

The Wonderful Power of Renunciation

8. "Renunciation is the consecration of worldly and spiritual duties to the Lord."

Renunciation may be external or internal. Both the objects and attachment to objects are objects from the self's point of view, but Narada is addressing an individual who does not know who he is. So it is important for this person to understand that whereas specific external objects can be renounced – you can let go of your job, house, wife and kids, for example – attachment to the idea that objects are necessary for your happiness is an obstacle to freedom and non-dual love. If you let go of the idea, you can keep the wife and kids because, present or absent, they are non-different from you.

Non-dual devotees – free people – are satisfied with themselves and consequently they have no worldly or spiritual goals. They do actions – who can avoid action even for a second? – but they have no attachment to the results, because they are already full. Certain actions are not optional – eating, sleeping and breathing, for instance – but many actions need not be done to ensure one's survival. People who feel that they are incomplete are always busy doing unnecessary actions for happiness's sake. For example, people want to fall in love. However, if you know who you are, this desire does not arise, because you are non-dual love. Why would you go out for hamburgers and beer when you have filet mignon and champagne at home in the refrigerator?

A milkman prayed for an inexhaustible source of milk so he could become rich. The Lord appeared and granted his wish. But the milkman was not satisfied, so he said, "As you perhaps know, Lord, I am in the habit of watering down my milk to make more money, so please give me an endless supply of water as well." Old habits die hard. We have an undying source of love at our disposal – love is the nature of the self – but we chase decaying experiences for love.

This is not to say that free non-dual devotees do not have desires, only that acting on them is completely optional. In addition to the power to act and to know, the power of desire is a sacred and glorious gift from God only bestowed on human beings. If you interview a dog about its plans, it may bark a couple of times and then run off to sniff the behind of another dog. But human beings can pursue extraordinary world-enhancing objectives, not the least of which is non-dual love.

The Wonderful Power of Desire

Knowing full well that fullness is his nature, the free non-dual wise person's cup runneth over. *Isvara's* desire to serve the creation courses through him, and his life is service, a declaration of *Isvara's* glory and undying love for the world. Even *Isvara* seems to enjoy Its "desires." As the *Taittiriya Upanishad* in this personified verse (2.6.1) says:

> "He desired and said, 'I will become many. I will father many children.' So He performed austerities and created everything, then appeared as everything seen and unseen in His creation."

Desire is harmless and wonderful, but only in service to *Isvara*. Without *Isvara*-knowledge it ties the self-ignorant to ignoble actions and creates ugly distorted egos attached to worldly, religious and spiritual identities. However, it does not bind non-dual devotees who are free of worldly and spiritual desires. Enlightenment sickness, the ego's identification with spiritual attainments, does not afflict the one who knows his nature is non-dual love.

A non-dual devotee is one who cannot be improved by doing anything. His life is dedicated solely to actualizing what he knows (*nididhyasana*). And what does he know? He knows that he is everything and everything is him, so there is no room for injurious thoughts and actions. All his relationships are love relationships. If I am love and everyone is me, what's not to love? These devotees enjoy wonderful lives because everything required to survive in the transactional reality comes from "others." If others are loved, they cannot help but love back – it is *Isvara's* law of *karma* – and so the world takes excellent care of such devotees.

Consecration Is Renunciation

Life is an attempt to satisfy an inexhaustible stream of desires and pander to an unending procession of fears. To thwart the unconscious recycling of fear and desire, Vedanta recommends converting desire into devotion by offering all one's actions and their results to God. Dedicated activities break rather than create attachments, turning the heart into a pure, luminous reflector of non-dual love. Since the devotee trusts God to dispense the fruits of his or her actions according to Its wisdom, the mind is free to settle down and inquire into the nature of the self.

The more we're attached to objects the less love we experience, and conversely, fewer attachments equals more love. The desire for ever-increasing love springs from *Isvara* urging us to consecrate the results of our actions. Desire, lust, anger, attachment, arrogance, acquisitiveness, possessiveness, sloth, greed, pride, etc. often seem so powerful we slavishly toady to them. Invariably we resist consecrating our actions and testily defend the fortress of rationalization and justification we've constructed to validate them. Occasionally, puffed with pride, we turn them into hard and fast credentials. Consequently devotees often believe that renunciation of the results is painful. Nothing could be further from the truth.

A rich and famous person, attracted to the simplicity of a devotee's life, said, "What a great soul you are, having given up everything in the world, yet you are so happy!" "No," the devotee replied, "you are much greater than me. I have only renounced worldly things for eternal love, but you've renounced eternal love for the goods of this world."

9. "Renunciation is one-pointed devotion to *Isvara* and complete indifference to objects."

I read a reasonable translation of this text that applies to the knowledge-seeking devotee saying that renunciation "requires" singular devotion to *Isvara* and complete indifference to objects. Renunciation born of appreciation of the zero-sum nature of duality may direct the heart to *Isvara* or not. If not, the seeker will undoubtedly remain as a *samsari* and will experience some version of a "dark night of the soul" because the mind needs a positive altar at which to worship. But if his attention is directed to *Isvara,* he will become inspired and uplifted as his God-knowledge becomes more and more refined. It is not possible to take one's attention away from objects unless there is a suitable alternative altar at which one can offer worship. Paying attention to *Isvara* is single-pointed devotion and is required for self-knowledge, which in turn is required for non-dual devotion. So in this case renunciation is the practice of keeping the mind on *Isvara.* Keeping the mind on *Isvara* develops dispassion, the number-one qualification for self-knowledge and non-dual devotion.

But the verse is actually a simple description of a non-dual devotee of whom nothing is required. The mind craves objects because objects seem to be beautiful. But an enlightened person is dispassionate because his attention is totally absorbed in *Isvara's* beauty, which is the source of the beauty reflected in objects. In this case dispassion is effortless and not the result of disciplining the mind to stay with *Isvara.* Knowledge of *Isvara,* not effort, keeps the non-dual devotee's mind on *Isvara.* Knowledge needs no maintenance. How does a dualistic devotee keep the mind on *Isvara*? By exposing the mind constantly to the teachings of Vedanta in the context of an introspective and *dharmic* life.

In the devotional schools, the idea of singular devotion amounts to sectarian fundamentalism, a "my God/your God" duality. In that strange dualistic world, my God is always better than your God. There is a sect of literalist Krishna devotees in India and abroad that ignores Krishna's non-dual statements in the *Gita* altogether and believes that singular devotion means fidelity to the god Krishna as opposed to all other gods. Somehow it seems lost on them that the word "*krsna*" means "what is always attractive," which can only be love. Love is the most sought-after experience in life and it is available to everybody everywhere. It knows no duality; it is one.

When God excludes everything else, God is effectively reduced to one of the finite beings in the creation. Dualists may think they are glorifying God, but they are actually degrading God with their concept of exclusivity.

The Definition of God

The word "God" suffers mightily for want of a definition. Without a definition, God can be whatever you want it to be, which may be convenient for believers but is not helpful for inquirers. In Vedanta, God is a nuanced concept. Since it refers to something empirical but unavailable for perception, the only access to understanding God is the logic presented in the scriptures, keeping in mind that inference is a valid means of knowledge.

If reality is a non-duality, then the self – uncreated, limitless, non-dual existence/consciousness – is God because there is no other option. However, how do we account for the world and conscious beings, which are definitely created and which, at first glance, do not seem to be uncreated, limitless, non-dual existence/consciousness? Vedanta accounts for the existence of objects with the concept of *Maya*. It says that there is a power in existence/consciousness, neither the same as it nor different from it, that creates the world and conscious beings, just as a person enjoys the power to create a work of art or a meal, for instance. The power is not separate from the person, but it is not identical with him either. So God is pure uncreated awareness plus *Maya,* the power to create. What does it create? It creates everything that exists.

Evil Belongs to Ignorance, Not to God

So Vedanta's definition of God is "everything that exists." Such a definition presents dualists with a problem: How can God be everything that exists, because everything that exists includes evil? We cannot blame them for this doubt, because they do not understand the concept of *Maya,* ignorance, which says that evil is the result of ignorance of the nature of God. In other words, evil is a projection of the human mind, not an actual fact. Humans are the only beings with this notion. Other conscious beings are mercifully spared thoughts about the moral value of creation. Concerning the role of uncreated awareness in its role as Creator, the *Bhagavad Gita* says: "I [awareness] am the cause of the entire universe and the entire universe is the effect," which we can take to mean: consciousness alone manifests in the form of everything. If *Isvara* includes everything, the idea of an exclusive God is ridiculous because it degrades God, reducing its status to that of a created finite object subject to birth and death. Every seeker, meaning every devotee, needs to understand that God includes material objects and sentient beings, but that no object is inherently good or evil.

In the *Bhagavad Gita* (7:4-5) God is presented as two principles: a higher principle (*para prakriti*) and a lower principle (*apara prakriti*). **Both are**

beginningless and eternal, but there are fundamental differences between them. The higher principle is the conscious principle (*chetana*), whereas the lower principle is inert matter (*achetana*); the higher one is without properties and attributes (*nirguna*), whereas the lower one has attributes and properties (*saguna*); the higher principle is not subject to change, as it is beyond time, whereas the lower one is subject to change, and time is its essence. Finally, the higher principle is independent (*satyam*), whereas the lower principle (*mithya*) is dependent upon the higher one. This spirit-matter mixture existed before the emergence or evolution of the universe, which is gradual, occurring in two stages. The higher principle remains unchanged from the beginning of creation when the mirror of matter appears and throughout all its stages. In the intermediate stage, however, matter or energy divides into eight sub-principles. In the final stage, the eightfold material nature magnifies and expands to become the multifarious creation consisting of everything: the galaxies, solar systems, planets, continents, the body (an assemblage of modified matter) and mind (subtle matter). Thus both body and mind are the final products of the lower principle.

The verse then enumerates the eightfold material principle in the intermediate stage. These consist of earth, water, fire, air, space (the five elements), as well as mind (*manas*), intellect (*buddhi*) and the "I"-sense (*ahankara*). It is important to note that the scriptures talk about two types of five elements: (1) the gross tangible or concrete elements that are the final products of evolution and (2) the subtle elements, which are intermediary objects. Verse 4 talks about the subtle elements, or intermediary objects – the invisible earth, water, fire, air and space principles, as well as the subtle mind, intellect and ego. The latter three are technical words based on Sankhyan cosmology and should not be mistaken for the human mind, intellect and ego. Rather they should be understood as the intermediary stages of these three matter principles which have to be established in the macrocosm before they can appear in the microcosm.

Then verse 5 introduces the higher principle, consciousness. According to scripture, both matter and energy, the lower principle, are "inferior" because they are inert and subject to change, whereas consciousness is "superior" or desirable because it is changeless. Consciousness is superior because people are seeking freedom from change, i.e. their bodies and minds; discovering "I am consciousness and not the body-mind" sets them free and delivers total security. Many people think consciousness is a kind of energy. The proponents of experiential enlightenment make this mistake because they seek experience and experience is just various patterns of subtle energy. But consciousness is not subject to modification, so it is neither matter nor energy. Then what is consciousness? It is simply ordinary, ever-present, always-experienced consciousness.

Therefore Krishna, speaking as consciousness, says: "May you know my higher nature, which is other than matter and energy and which is beyond scientifically observable physical and chemical laws." So wherever you look in the creation you will only discover changing objects, which you can rule out as the self, eliminating the body and mind and every observable and experienceable thing. You may argue, as atheists do, that eliminating everything observable and experienceable leaves nothing, and erroneously conclude that there is no superior principle in the creation. Your argument would not hold up, however, because you are excluding your self, the conscious observer of change. The creation is simply a mixture of a single, conscious, unchanging subject and continuously changing objects. So look to yourself; the changing part is not-you and the changeless part is you. When the unchanging awareness that you are shines on the inert matter part of you, your body and mind are enlivened. You lend life to them, not they to you.

The entire universe is sustained by consciousness. At the physical body level, consciousness is experienced as the very life principle (*prana*). If you have any doubt, touch your body and you will experience sentience, proving that it is blessed by the conscious principle. But if you are no longer associated with your body, it becomes food for worms. If you extend this reasoning to the cosmic level, you can only conclude that the cosmos is one harmonious intelligent being. The visible, experienceable part of the creation is matter, and the intelligent sustaining principle is God, consciousness.

Devotional practice is always meaningful, but devotional literature only becomes truly meaningful when you have knowledge of God. Since God includes everything, no object, sentient or insentient, can be excluded. Dualists therefore are not interested in Vedanta's knowledge of God, as there is no way to distinguish their god from other's gods, thus robbing them of their sense of superiority.

Four Types of Devotees

One-pointed devotion (*anaya bhakti*) is a technical term that describes the type of devotion practiced by the knowledge-seeking devotee and the self-realized devotee, not the suffering or desiring devotee.

For the knowledge-seeker, there is no goal other than God, or *moksa*. His devotion manifests as a burning desire for freedom. God is freedom because it is totally disassociated from the matter principle, which is the cause of bondage. The self-realized devotee worships devotion itself. He is in love with love and knows that his nature is love. He can confidently say, "I am love." In the context of these verses this verse refers to the self-realized person's devotion because the topic is non-dual devotion. In addition to seeing God as non-different from myself, the non-dual devotee is "completely indifferent to objects," meaning contrary to *Isvara* – and scripture. In Vedanta, we do not differentiate between *Isvara* and scripture, which is *Isvara* revealing Itself by unfolding the unexamined logic of existence to the human mind.

Since non-dual devotees live in a world of rampant materialism where atheism abounds, what is his attitude to unbelievers? He is indifferent to those who don't accept God and even those who hate God.

Hate the Sin, Not the Sinner

The non-dual devotee doesn't hate anyone, not even terrorists. He strongly condemns evil actions and is happy to avoid or fight wrongdoers – it is his duty to uphold *dharma* – but he is indifferent to them because he understands that if they could be different, they would be different. As Krishna says (*Bhagavad Gita*, 12.13):

> "My devotee is a non-hater of all. He is friendly, compassionate and free from the 'I and mine' notion. He is forbearing, the same in comfortable and uncomfortable circumstances."

If at all we have something to say about ungodly *adharmic* people, we pray that their minds become purified. Shankaracharya gives a lovely example of this in *Vivekachudamani*. A piece of sandalwood has a delightful smell, but if it is in a damp environment, moss grows on it and it emanates a foul odor; nobody would believe it is fragrant. But if the moss is scraped off and the sandalwood rubbed on a rough rock, its lovely fragrance fills the air. *Adharmis* are actually non-separate from God; they are just contaminated by self-ignorance. Consequently they are selfish, egoic, vain, materialistic, possessive and deluded. Don't hate them – "there but for the grace of God go I" – but keep your distance. Here is a wonderful prayer:

> "May the wicked become good, may the good attain peace, may the peaceful attain liberation and may the liberated help to set others free. May all beings be happy and free from disease. May everyone find what they seek and no one experience sorrow. May the rains fall on time, the earth abundantly yield its bounty and may we all be free from fear. May all beings cross over their tribulations and accomplish their aims. May everyone in every place, at all times, be happy."

10. "When devotion is one-pointed, the devotee only seeks security in the self."
As already mentioned, one-pointed devotion is non-sectarian. Sectarianism is an unfortunate phenomenon, as it leads to fundamentalism, which is pure duality, not to mention the Crusades and ISIS. There is no way to quarrel if there is only God. If you understand that there is only God and God is love, you will love everyone equally.

No Way to Quarrel if There Is Only God

The knowledge-seeking devotee is not captivated by the beauty, variety and novelty of the world, because he is well aware of the downside, its lack of security. Therefore, owing to his knowledge of God, he relies only on God for security because God is always present and unchanging and God is what everyone wants: freedom and unconditional love. This devotee is secure in the knowledge that whatever life brings comes from *Isvara* for a good reason and is therefore content with everything that happens. He loves everyone in his life and helps them, but when it comes to emotional support he doesn't lean on them; he leans on *Isvara*. As Krishna (*Bhagavad Gita,* 9.22) says:

> "Those who see me as non-different from them offer worship by dwelling on me. I take care of the getting and keeping of those ever-steadfast souls."

I know a spiritual woman from a rich materialistic family who was looked down upon by her relatives for her lack of interest in financial security. When asked how she supported herself, she said, "I have God's trust fund." Even though this type of devotee has progressed from world-dependence to God-dependence, God is still remote, so one more step remains. By contrast, the self-realized devotee knows that God is the "self residing in the heart of all beings." (*Bhagavad Gita,* 10:20) In this person, God-dependence is self-dependence. But depending on the self alone is not dependence; it is freedom and unconditional love. There is nothing left to do for someone who loves only the self, is contented with the self alone.

The Five Stages of Devotion

This summary of Chapter XII on devotion in the *Bhagavad Gita* unfolds the five stages of love that culminate in liberation. It is comparable to the first chapter of these *Bhakti Sutras*.

Love makes the world go around. Our efforts to attain objects are based on the desire to please the self. We want to please ourselves because we love ourselves. Because reality is non-dual, knowledge and love are one, but there is a persistent and uninformed notion in the spiritual world that knowledge has nothing to do with love. However, just as time and space are two different ways to measure the distance from one object to another, knowledge and love are just two interconnected ways of measuring one's distance from or proximity to one's self.

Stage 1: Praying for Stuff - *Sakama Bhakti* [7]

Karma yoga is love *yoga* because it coverts a worldly life into a spiritual life. I practice it because I love a quiet mind. I love a quiet mind because discrimination – which is tantamount to freedom – only works when the mind is reasonably clear. Discrimination reveals the ever-free love that I am. Freedom is unconditional self-love.

In this stage, the devotee initially uses *Isvara* as a multi-purpose agent to whom he assigns a variety of tasks. His problems are shunted off on *Isvara* and, if possible, *Isvara* should produce a few miracles into the bargain. Vedanta is not against the miracle-mongering indicative of this stage, but devotees need to work out of this state of mind as quickly as possible. Miracles do not make the devotee spiritually exceptional. Vedanta transcends miracles and mysticism. Vedanta proves this statement: you are the authority that validates every experience. What greater miracle – a fact, actually – could there be than this?

It is a struggle to take one's angers and disappointments as a gift from God when devotion is selfish. Like a child, the devotee begs and whines, "I need a new X." Or, if he or she is business-minded, "I will chant your holy name one thousand times if you see to it that my son passes his English exam." This kind of devotion is not sophisticated or particularly noble, but

[7] See chart above Stage 2.

it reveals a rudimentary desire to relate to God; we have to start somewhere. However, devotion for God's stuff does not remove anxiety and depression. At least there is a basic understanding that God – the field of existence – is responsible for delivering objects, and a feeble attempt to accept God's will.

In this stage, if the person is seeking God – whatever that means to him – he may mechanically repeat his favorite name of God without understanding who he is talking to. Or, because he is *tamasic* and prone to fantasy, he may believe that one circumambulation of the holy mountain Arunachala on a full-moon night or one million repetitions of a special *mantra* is sufficient for *moksa*. This kind of devotion is often encouraged in the *Puranas*. In fact although it is the lowest form of devotion, it is touted as the highest form in the last verse of Chapter XII just to encourage beginners. The way out of this stage is to pray for the well-being of others.

Stage 2: Breeding Ground for Saints - *Nishkama Bhakti*[8]

In this stage, desire for worldly things is not allowed, only prayer for the courage and strength to take both positive and negative results as a gift from *Isvara,* i.e. the law of *karma*. The devotee is not aiming for a particular experience. There is desire, but the desire is for peace of mind. This stage purifies likes and dislikes because one goes with what *Isvara,* one's situation, demands, not what one wants. The devotee stops treating God as a problem-solver, takes his *karma* like a man and stops blaming God for his bad *karma*.

"Selfless" Service

Obviously, from the non-dual perspective any action is the self giving service to itself, but in the second stage the extroverted devotee is trying to purify selfishness, so he asks God to help others, not himself. This stage breeds saints. Serving the world is as good as serving God because the world is God. It is not an easy stage, because the devotee is praying for the strength to resist worldly desires. In the first stage, you may have realized that desiring objects isn't healthy, but you are still attached to them. At the same time, you know that to see God your heart must be pure. Devotees in this stage staff monasteries, churches and temples and do a rudimentary form of *karma yoga* without understanding the nuances of its logic. Since the *karma* they do accrues to the accounts of others, they don't accumulate *vasanas* – except the *vasana* for service, which can bind like any other. Most large spiritual and religious organizations are

[8]See chart above Stage 3.

built on the backs of this kind of devotee. They believe that when all their *karmas* are burned up by action, enlightenment will ensue. On the kitchen wall of a very wealthy *ashram* I observed this sign: "One hour of dishwashing burns one lifetime of *karma*"! They do not understand that action won't burn ignorance and that *moksa* burns the doer in the fire of self-knowledge.

Stage 3: My Personal Deity - *Istha Devata Abyasa* [9]

Inner Work – Meditation

The *karma yoga* stages convert an extroverted mind into an introverted mind. In the meditation phase there is a gradual reduction of worldly activities and an increase of mental activity. Because one's thoughts are now going to a symbol of the self, symbols invoke their referents and the self is unconditional love (*parama prema*), the devotee experiences love without reference to objects and events. In this stage, the devotee bonds with *Isvara* and nourishes his relationship with *Isvara*. He no longer depends on relationships for love – family and friends – but draws on *Isvara* for emotional support. This stage removes fear.

The goal of spiritual life is to see God, the self, in everything, but non-dual vision – which amounts to non-dual love – requires a very subtle mind. At this stage the devotee's mind is not expansive enough to gain that vision, so he or she worships a specific symbol of God that stands for the total, an *ishta devata*.

It is okay to do this because every object is actually non-separate from the total, although it seems to be. Chapter X of the *Bhagavad Gita* presents a list of particularly exceptional, beautiful and awesome manifestations of God which are easy to worship: the sun, the Himalayas, great saints, magnificent animals, the brilliance in a brilliant mind, preternatural human beauty, etc. One need only recognize the objects that elevate one's mind, the night sky, for instance, and diligently contemplate their origin. As the name for this type of worship implies, devotion is related to one's personal tastes, so likes and dislikes are still operating. Mental and physical actions and their results are dedicated to one's personal deity – Jesus, Allah, Mother Mary, Krishna, Shiva, angels, etc.

Stage 4: Worship of Everything - *Visvat Swarupa* [10]

Removing Likes and Dislikes

This, the penultimate stage, further expands and purifies the mind. It removes likes and dislikes: jealousy, hatred, possessiveness, etc. There is still duality

[9]See chart above Stage 3. [10]See chart above Stage 4.

- relationship - in this stage, but the "person" to whom one relates is the conscious being that is everything.

Seeing the divinity in particular objects that excite one's love for God is well and good, but seeing the divine in all objects is the goal. In this stage the devotee must drill down into every object appearing in his consciousness until he can see consciousness - his own innermost self - shining there. Chapter XI of the *Bhagavad Gita* presents the self in its creative aspect as a cosmic universal person, someone that is both wonderful and terrifying, the idea being that the devotee should love the ugly, angry, fearful parts of his or her self and accept the evil in the world as an inevitable consequence of self-ignorance. The holy parts of one's self are easy to love, the dark parts less so. As long as differences exist in the devotee's mind, love is conditional.

Emotional Impact, the "Vision" of the Total

The purpose of this vision is to instill a sense of reverence and love for everything because everything is nothing but the self of the devotee. Seeing objects in this way removes one's likes and dislikes. The vision of everything as one's self gives rise to wonderment in the devotee: How can a thing and its opposite be just one thing, my self? It also generates fear because it involves the acceptance of the inevitable losses - the death of love-objects: the body and one's family - that are part and parcel of the fabric of life. It is complete when the devotee overcomes his fears and happily accepts the inevitable demise of all objects, particularly the body and loved ones.

At this stage, the devotee sees every action as worship of the Lord and does not care about the results of actions, because his sole purpose it to arrive at Stage 5.

Stage 5: The Fruit of Devotion - Non-Duality [11]

Jnana Yoga Is Non-Dual Love

In this stage, the devotee realizes that *Isvara* and *Jiva* enjoy the same identity, which destroys the relationship between the individual and the world. You are me and I am you. Everything is me. I am love.

Enlightened devotees are free from mental and emotional events created by desire. They have no desire for objects, because they are full. They can fulfill the desires of others because they are non-binding. They are here to serve. They are emotionally tolerant and do not disapprove of those who

[11] See chart above Stage 4.

do not conform to their values. They are free of possessiveness because they understand that everything belongs to *Isvara*. They are not seduced by *Maya's* beauty, variety and novelty. They are free from arrogance, pride, superiority and competitiveness. They get along with everyone and everyone gets along with them because they have fragrant, compassionate personalities. Everything they do adds value to life.

To summarize the summary: there are two levels of *karma yoga,* two levels of *upasana yoga* and one level of *jnana yoga.* Taken together, these five levels comprise devotional *yoga.*

Evolution of Devotional Knowledge

Devotional knowledge evolves in this way: first, we believe in **(1) God in one form**, a remote, personal God (*paroksha Isvara*) with humanlike characteristics subject to intermittent appearances in response to a devotee's longing or to save the devotee from a crisis. Next, we come to appreciate **(2) God in many forms,** an immediately available, directly-experienced God *(pratakshya Isvara)* in the form of the objects that present themselves to our consciousness. In fact the *Uddhava Gita* presents the whole universe as the first incarnation of consciousness. Therefore everything we experience from womb to tomb is God. Finally, we are set free when we realize that we are non-different from **(3) an imperceptible but immediately known God** (*aparoksha Isvara*), not different from myself, which is:

> "That which speech cannot express, but that by which it is possible to speak is the Supreme and not what the world reveres. That which the mind cannot know, but by which the mind is known is the Supreme and not what the world reveres. That which the eye cannot see, but which peers through eye is the Supreme and not what the world reveres. That which the ear cannot hear, but which makes hearing possible is the Supreme and not what this world reveres. That which the living breath does not inspire, but which inspires the living breath - know this to be the Supreme and not what the world reveres." (*Kena Upanishad,* 1.5-1.9)

It is:

> "That which is never seen, but which witnesses everything; that which is never heard, but is the essence of the hearer; that which is never thought, but thinks the thinker; that which is never known, but is the knower of the known and the unknown. There is no other witness, no other hearer, no other thinker, no other knower. This inner ruler is your own immortal self. Everything else is merely mortal." (*Brihadaranyaka Upanishad,* 3.7.23)

No Skipping!

I'm writing these commentaries in the middle of winter in the mountains of Western Oregon. Each morning when I start the fire, there are hot coals left over from the previous night. If I throw a large log on the coals, it will not ignite. I need to put paper, cardboard, small kindling, then larger pieces and finally, the log on top. The fire needs to work though the various kindling points until it is hot enough to ignite the log. Similarly, anyone who wants to attain *moksa* will necessarily have to go through all four devotional levels to attain the fifth, freedom and non-dual love. If you do not complete the course, you will be subject to suffering.

As mentioned previously, *Isvara* has a lower nature and a higher, formless nature. To erase the duality in his devotion and find peace, a devotee must eventually come to understand the formless nature of God,[12] which Krishna describes in two very brilliant and important verses in the twelfth chapter of the *Bhagavad Gita* (12.3-4):

> "Having restrained the sense organs, being even-minded towards all and interested in the welfare of all beings, some devotees meditate upon the imperishable consciousness, which is indefinable, unmanifest, all-pervading, incomprehensible, immutable, immoveable and eternal. They alone attain me."

Then, in the next verse (12.5), he says:

> "Difficulties are greater for those whose minds are committed to the pursuit of the unmanifest (*brahman*), for the goal of

[12]See chart Stage 5.

> the unmanifest is difficult to attain by those who are attached to the idea that they are the body."

Thus the highest level of devotion *yoga* requires inquiry and analysis into formless consciousness, and is difficult for those who are attached to objects, the body particularly. However, we should not avoid inquiry because it is difficult. If it is difficult, the only conclusion to be drawn is that you should stop worrying about liberation and prepare your mind for it. When the heart and mind are ready, the non-dual teachings, which transform dualistic devotion to non-dual devotion, make perfect sense.

Because inquiry is difficult for the unqualified mind, devotees would naturally like some evidence that it actually works, much as we insist that new medicines should be tested on others before we test them on ourselves. The *Gita* assures us that many have practiced inquiry and attained freedom, and gives a brilliant description of the non-dual devotee, who is called the "supreme" devotee, "My devotee, a non-hater of all beings, is friendly, compassionate and devoid of the notion of 'I and mine.' He or she is forbearing; the same in comfortable and uncomfortable situations." (12:13)

Although the non-dual devotee takes care of all beings in the beautiful, variegated, ever-novel creation, he never depends on anyone for his happiness, because he is supremely self-satisfied.

11. "Devotees with one-pointed devotion perform only worldly and religious duties that are in harmony with *dharma*."

In Sanskrit a renunciant is called a *sannyasi.*[13] Renunciants who are

[13]There are four types of *sannyasa,* based on the nature of renunciation, ranging from partial to total. The highest form of *sannyasa* is *paramahamsa sannyasa,* which is the renunciation of everything, and there are "lower-grade" *sannyasis* who still have an interest in something worldly. *Paramahamsa sannyasa* is further subdivided into two types: *vividisha sannyasa* and *vidvat sannyasa. Vividisha sannyasa* is undertaken for scriptural study. *Vividisha* means "desiring to know" (see the end of "'Selfless' Service," page 50). *Vividisha sannyasa* is a step toward *vidvat sannyasa,* in which a *sannyasi* is no longer interested in anything. He has attained the knowledge and does not hold onto anything, not even to the idea "I am a *jnani.*" He does not even have pride in the knowledge. Thus the aim of *vividisha sannyasa* is committed scriptural study, and the aim of *vidvat sannyasa* is total renunciation. According to the *Vedas, vividisha sannyasa* is the ideal means and *vidvat sannyasa* is the ideal end in life. Why is this the case? If someone wants an empirical model for the self, a *sannyasi* serves as such a model because the self is free of all actions and duties. He does not have family duties, social duties, religious duties, a duty to earn,

not comfortable in worldly lifestyles can either go to an *ashram* to study Vedanta systematically under the guidance of a *guru* to get firm self-knowledge or they can gain non-dual devotion as a householder. However, a householder can practice listening, reasoning and actualizing, but he or she will have to make appropriate lifestyle adjustments to do so.

Although a householder non-dual devotee is not required to follow householder customs and duties, the verse says he should execute them properly. If

Footnote continued from page 49...

etc. Second, the *Vedas* say that self is free from all relations. Similarly, in taking *sannyasa,* the *sannyasi* breaks all relationships. Third, the self is behind everything, supporting everything. Like the self, the *sannyasi* supports the whole creation. He does not belong to anyone; he belongs to everyone. Nothing belongs to him; everything belongs to everyone. Fourth, the self does not depend upon anything for security, and neither does a *sannyasi.* He does not have a bank balance, a house, etc. He finds security in himself. The beauty is that he gives security to others, and the irony is that the other person to whom he gives security could be a very rich person, while the *sannyasi* himself is a pauper. This *vividisha sannyasa* is the ideal means. *Sannyasa* is also the ideal end. In renunciation alone does one achieve mastery. A *sannyasi* gives up everything that will inevitably be snatched away in time or at death. The only unsnatchable entity is the self. The Vedantin's approach is this: when something is snatched away from us, the sense of loss is intensified; when it is given up or given away by us, the pleasure is intensified. There was a lady who, while visiting the temple, lost a gold ornament. She thought somebody had stolen it. She became very upset and took an oath that if the ornament were to be found, she would offer it to the Lord. As it turned out, she found the ornament and offered it to the Lord, which made her very happy. When she had lost the ornament, she lost the benefit of wearing it and was very sad, but when she gave the ornament to the Lord, even as she lost the benefit of wearing it, she was very happy. This example illustrates that both in loss and in giving we are without an object, but whereas in loss there is pain, in giving there is pleasure. So we hand it over to time before time takes it away from us. This way, when things go – whether money, relationships or our hair and teeth in old age – we do not feel any pain. A renunciant is not worried about losing anything, including his body. He knows that time is going to take everything away. He holds onto just one thing that time cannot take away: the self. He can even challenge death because he knows that death cannot touch him. So what is the ultimate renunciation? Giving up everything that can be lost or taken away and finding security in what cannot be snatched. This is called *paramahamsa sannyasa* or *vidvat sannyasa.* What is the life of such a *sannyasi*? Because he does not belong to any particular family or community, he keeps moving from place to place. If he remains in one place, there is a danger that he may get attached to people and that people may get attached to him. His life is to teach. He does not have anything; he does not know what his security will be tomorrow. Yet he seems to be the happiest person. When we see such a *sannyasi,* we come to recognize that we don't need things for joy.

you are in a relationship of any sort, even though you desire to leave, you need to follow leaving-*dharma*. For example, if you want to leave your husband or wife because they are indifferent to or non-supportive of your spiritual life, you should not just abruptly walk away even though you are beyond all prohibitions and injunctions; you should tidy up your *karma* first.

Three Reasons Enlightened People Should Follow *Dharma*

Narada presents three important reasons why the non-dual devotee should follow rules and regulations, both secular and sacred.

1. Protection of Society

When your self-knowledge is unassailable and your love of the self and the creation is unconditional, you understand very clearly that the *Jiva*-self owes an incredible lifelong debt to God. Until that time, there is always a feeling that you are here in human form to get something, which is true, but not the whole truth. We have been put here by God to contribute our talents, skills and love to the creation. *Karma yoga* is an attempt to get an immature, small, self-centered person to acknowledge his indebtedness to God in the form of the world and to happily discharge that debt.

Follow the Rules

Narada says that with regard to both secular and sacred scriptural activities – from traffic rules to The Ten Observances (*niyamas*) – may you live in accordance with Vedic injunctions and prohibitions. Despite the fact that a self-realized person is unaffected when he violates rules, he should dot his "i"s and cross his "t"s. Enlightened people can be compared to children. If a child violates the rules, the child is not arrested. Similarly, when a cow walks onto the road, violating the traffic signal, the traffic police don't ask for its license and registration and write a ticket. Rules are relevant only where ego is involved. A non-dual devotee has transcended the doer-enjoyer entity – he is the self after all, so even if he violates the rules, he will not accrue good or bad *karma*. As it says in *Tattva Bodha* (verse 38.1):

> "Knowledge destroys future *karma*, and the self-realized person is not affected by it, just as a lotus leaf is not affected by drops of water sitting on it."

So even though a non-dual devotee is not afraid of bad *karma,* he or she nonetheless follows the rules, not out of a desire for good *karma* or fear of punishment, but out of compassion for the worldly order.

> "Just as ignorant people act with attachment to action, a wise person should act without attachment and a desire to bring about the upliftment of society. The wise should not create confusion in the minds of ignorant people attached to action. Efficiently performing all duties with discipline, the wise person should inspire others." (*Bhagavad Gita,* 3.25-26)

Not only should you perform helpful actions, they should be performed with utmost commitment. Don't do a sloppy job just because you don't require the benefit. Anything worth doing is worth doing well. Therefore may you maintain *dharma* and help society. We can learn the *dharmic* way of life from Vedanta, which informs us who we are and tells us how to live in accordance with self-knowledge and secondary Vedic texts (*smriti*)[14] such as the *Itihasas, Puranas* and *Dharma Shastras,* and modeling our lives on the lives of proper *mahatmas.* Just as children learn how to live, eat, walk and talk by watching their parents' example, every enlightened person living in the world should know that he or she is a role model.

At the same time, a wise non-dual devotee should be indifferent, not disdainful, of actions contrary to *dharma.* Self-realized persons should be ready to share their knowledge and help anyone that is open-minded and willing to do the work. It is pointless to talk to someone who is not ready to listen. When people are unreceptive, simply ignore them or, at most, pray for them.

12. "Firmly commit yourself to maintaining an ethical code even after your devotion to *Isvara*/God is firm."

It is a common-sense natural law that if you are protected by something, you have a responsibility to protect it in return. Parents look after their children, and children should look after their parents when they become incapable of looking after themselves. For someone who wants freedom – and who

[14]To-be-remembered histories, the most important being the *Bhagavad Gita, Ramayana* and *Mahabharata.* In these texts the "gods" are thinly veiled symbols of enlightened human beings. Owing to this literature, which presents the *Vedas* in code, Vedanta was never lost, because although the direct teachings were concealed, common people could learn how enlightenment affects one's behavior.

doesn't? – Vedanta is the means. It protects us from ignorance and teaches us how to live and inquire. If I get the benefit – freedom and non-dual love – it is my sacred duty to protect and perpetuate it.

2. Protection of Scripture

1. Live a stand-up life. Freedom is not license to do whatever you want. Self-realized people who violate *dharma* – vulgar and uncultured crazy-wisdom *gurus,* for instance – are little more than animals. Until you know who you are and your knowledge is firm, scripture is your protection. But once you know, the roles are reversed and you need to protect scripture. A cultured person puts others first. We live on a river that is the habitat for many ducks and geese. Invariably, when a gaggle of geese lands on our lawn to eat the tender shoots of grass, one or two large ganders forgo eating to keep watch while the others eat.

If a free, non-dual devotee were to regress and become a licentious, undisciplined, uncultivated, uncouth person, Vedanta would earn a bad name. Sadly, one of the reasons I have tried to eliminate many of the obvious signs of Vedic culture from Vedanta is due to the tremendous disservice to the idea of liberation visited on seekers by many Hindu *swamis* and their Western "disciples" who, since the sixties, have come to the West and severely tarnished its reputation: Osho/Rajneesh, Swami Satchitananda, Adi Da (a Hindu clone), Swami Muktananda, Yogi Amrit Desai, Andrew Cohen, Swami Sudananda (even in our lineage) and other small fish too numerous to mention. So it is our duty to teach by precept – AND EXAMPLE.

Indeed, Krishna argues this point in the *Bhagavad Gita*: "Arjuna, because you are a role model, if you run away from the battlefield, society will follow your example." And then he goes on to say, "Consider my case: I don't have anything to accomplish in life, because I know who I am, but as a human being I have come to the world for a reason and I am following my duty." Therefore the first aspect of scriptural protection is: an enlightened non-dual devotee should glorify the tradition, not bring disrepute to it.

2. Share the knowledge. Only wise non-dual devotees are properly qualified to teach. If they don't teach, seekers will be stuck with the perennially available and untutored crop of so-called teachers of enlightenment, who basically end up sharing ignorance and confusion in the form of the many enlightenment myths. If pure non-dual devotees shy away from teaching, we would wind up with several dead ends in the lineage. Therefore the scripture says to every truly enlightened person: don't neglect sincere seekers. As Shankaracharya says in *Vivekachudamani,* verse 41:

> "The great sage looked at the seeker with compassion and urged him to abandon fear now that he had taken refuge in him."

3. Self-Protection

If we don't regularly polish the brass and silver valuables in our homes, they become tarnished. Similarly, a non-dual devotee is advised to remain conversant with the scripture for the protection of his or her own self-knowledge.

Before you know who you are and attain non-dual devotion, you need to understand *Isvara* because knowledge of *Isvara* reveals why you cannot consider yourself to be a doer of action, the most hardwired manifestation of self-ignorance. In fact one definition of freedom is freedom from the doer because the doer is an object in you, awareness. On the other hand, you are ceaselessly active until the day you die and you continually think the thought, "I will do, I want to do, I should do, I could do, I did, etc." Thinking you are the cause of action is called "doership." When you understand *Isvara,* all the constituents of action, you can plainly see that you are not doing anything. But, ignorance being what it is, there is invariably an implied meaning of this teaching that realized souls often fail to investigate, to wit if I am free, I am free not to do anything or, alternatively, to do anything I want. If this view is not investigated, Narada's statement that you should maintain contact with the scripture may seem to impose a limitation on your freedom. Why should I keep up my relationship with the scripture?

13. "Because [as long a the notion of doership is present] there is the danger of a fall."

Enlightenment Sickness

When someone realizes who they are there is a natural tendency to ring the bell and get everyone to come to church. In fact the spiritual world is littered with the corpses of fallen *yogis* due to this idea. When you rediscover your freedom, the milk of non-dual kindness flows sweetly in your veins and you want to "share." You are glorious, radiant and ever so inspired, and you imagine that a mere glance from your compassionate eyes or a blast of loving energy from your amazing heart is sufficient to enlighten the masses. No blame, but even after gaining self-knowledge, a non-dual devotee must not become complacent or overconfident, because *Maya* is constantly pulling on him. Temptations – fame, power, pleasure, wealth or just the lure of a glorious new identity – The Self! – are many. The scriptures prescribe several rules for saving the enlightened from temptation. If caution is thrown to the wind, you are undoubtedly heading for a downfall, which does not mean losing self-knowledge, because once it is gained clearly and thoroughly it cannot be lost. Nonetheless, it can be overshadowed by egoism, ownership, false pride, attachment to sense pleasures and any number of worldly tendencies, particularly the desire for recognition.

Enlightenment calls for increased vigilance of one's values because it is much easier to gain worldly things when you know who you are than before. And entanglement with worldly things causes problems for enlightened and unenlightened *jivas* alike.

14. "For as long as the body lasts, one should minimally engage in worldly activities and only perform those actions necessary to sustain the body."

Less Is More

Previously, we talked about the qualitative importance of worldly behavior and activities in keeping with worldly and scriptural duties, but they should be quantitatively appropriate as well. We can't avoid the world altogether, because minimum transactions are required to maintain the body. However, fewer worldly activities means greater peace of mind. Serving the world is wonderful, but leave enough time for your own *dharma*, especially for continuing to integrate the knowledge into your life until you become completely satisfied with the self alone. Until the day you die, even if you are a great sage, you should allot sufficient time for Vedanta – reading, writing, sharing, meditating, etc. – because the *vasanas* of desire, anger, greed and sensual indulgence are waiting in the wings, always ready to burst onto the stage of your life to create drama.

> "If you dwell on sense objects, a fancy toward them arises. From fanciful obsessions, desire is born. From desire, anger arises. Anger causes delusion and loss of memory. If you can't remember why you are here, you lose your discrimination. An undiscriminating person is spiritually lost." (*Bhagavad Gita*, 2.62-63)

Informal and Formal Dualistic Devotion

Dualistic devotion is converted to non-dual devotion by self-inquiry. A devotee who practices informal dualistic devotion does not follow scriptural rules but expresses love of God in his or her own way, at times even violating scriptural rules. The formal dualistic devotee does *karma yoga* and *upasana yoga,*[15] which involves the "five great sacrifices." The informal devotee forms an emotional bond with a personal God and expresses it in a variety of ways that bring joy. The formal devotee does not take God personally but sees God in everything. All experienced objects and situations are taken to be the Lord.

The informal devotee needs to get into a particular state of mind to contact his or her personal deity, but when the formal devotee does *puja* to a symbol of the self, which he or she should do daily irrespective of his or her state of mind, each aspect of the worship represents worship of the whole cosmos. For instance, when sandalwood paste is applied to a symbol of the self, it means that the devotee appreciates the fact that the earth itself is God. When flowers are offered, he sees space – which is everywhere – as God. The water offering underpins an appreciation of *Isvara* as all the water on the earth. When the candle is lit, the fire element – the stars or a hot day, for instance – is seen as God. Wafting the incense stick before the deity reminds the devotee that the all-pervading air principle is God.

Formal devotion takes the devotee's love away from his or her subjective situation and converts it into an appreciation of the harmony of the principles that govern the macrocosmos, which are the glory of God alone. The rising sun is the glory of God. Fog in the morning, the rains or water evaporating on a hot summer day are the glory of God. *Isvara*-devotion is an intellectual, reverential admiration of the whole creation, not an emotional outpouring.

In the informal devotional stage, there is a conscious criticism of the world as a veil of tears. To deal with suffering the devotee disassociates from the world, fantasizes a personal God and lives in an inner world dominated by his creation. This inner God – dead *gurus* serve the same function – has one salient characteristic: it always tells the devotee what it wants to hear and never challenges its spiritual fantasies, which are legion. *Karma yoga* corrects the obsessive small-self-regard that motivates personal devotion by expanding the devotee's knowledge of God. It attempts to address the universal need to blame the world for one's failures – and the subsequent lack of self-esteem that it creates – by helping the devotee to understand the futility of taking

[15]See chart Stages 3 and 4.

responsibility for the results of actions that are never in the hands of the devotee in the first place. In other words, it creates an orderly *karma* stream by bringing *Isvara* into the devotee's daily outer life. Often those who live in an inner devotional state are bedeviled by numerous worldly problems. In the *upasana* stage, there is only a tiny remnant of subjectivity; the devotee is finally growing up, developing an intellectual appreciation of everything as the wonderful body of God. He does not hate anything, does not want to own anything and is happy with whatever life brings. He does not have to wait for Sunday to worship, because he sees God everywhere every day. The sunrise is enough. A Vedic hymn, the *Rudram,* says:

> "The Lord is the auspicious ruddy sunrise, the golden morning light, the brilliant white light of midday and the variegated hues of sunset. With our worship of the sun we pacify untold worldly angers."

Be God and Experience God

A dualistic devotee, who enjoys both emotional joy through worship of *Isvara* in a specific form and intellectual joy through *Isvara* in all forms, may resist the idea of *moksa* because it brings about non-dual devotion, which seems to imply the loss of the experiential joy associated with dualistic devotion. Do the very words "non-dual" lose their meaning – like "hot ice cream" – since the very idea of devotion implies duality, a lover and a beloved?

Dualistic devotees who are hostile to non-duality often justify their devotion with the following statement: "Why would I want to be God when I can experience God?" Aside from the fact that God can't be experienced as an object – unless it is thought to be a belief or an experience – reality is set up in such a way that it is quite possible to be God and experience God. You can be God because God is existence – being. As being you are free of discrete objective experiences, although as being/existence you experience yourself as existing. Nobody doubts that they exist. The moment you think, "I am," you acknowledge that you are God. Even to doubt that you exist, you have to exist. Furthermore, nothing needs to be done to make you exist, nothing needs to be done to maintain your existence and nothing can take existence away from you. At the same time, thanks to *Maya/Isvara,* you – existence – appear as an existent experiencing entity, a person who transacts with existent objects. The existence in the experiencing entity, the existent objects and you are one. It is a matter of experience and common knowledge that there are not two or more existences. So you are experiencing God whenever you experience objects – which is always. Therefore the idea that you need to forgo the experience of God as an experience to be God is totally illogical. You can't become God – existence – because you already are God. You only fear the loss of individuality because you don't understand that the individual is actually God appearing as someone else.

The clever argument that duality is superior to non-duality doesn't hold water. Dualistic devotees cite this example: they say, "Do you want to be sugar (*Isvara*) or do you want to taste sugar? If you become sugar then you cannot taste it, therefore you should want to be different from it so you can enjoy it." A non-dualist will reply in this way: "The desire to taste sugar is natural, but how can you taste it without becoming one with it?"

What is experientially true of objects is also true of *Isvara*. When you experience *Isvara,* you become one with *Isvara* and *Isvara* apparently becomes one with you, so the joy is in the merging. Yes, epiphanies are blissful, but they have the misfortune of being finite. When you taste sugar, you don't cease to exist; only the taster ceases to exist for the moment. If you ceased to exist, you wouldn't know you were tasting sugar. When you taste the bliss of the self, you are only removing a barrier that apparently separates you from yourself, not gaining something you don't enjoy always. The sugar just opened up a door to the bliss of your own nature. Non-duality is not the opposite of duality. They are in different orders of you, existence/consciousness. *Isvara* is the conscious part of your self that does not enjoy differences. So let go of the experiencer and embrace *Isvara*.

Non-dual devotion is the love of a self-realized devotee toward God, which has been discovered to be the devotee's essential nature. If God is everywhere, everything and always present, there can be no separation between the devotee and God. Non-dual devotion is self-love in which the self is *Isvara* itself. Self-love is never illogical, because whether you know it or not, everyone already loves his or her self, as stated above and repeatedly stated in the *Upanishads*.

The proof of the scriptures' many statements that all love is self-love lies in the simple fact that all our actions are intended to please ourselves. Nobody intentionally sets out to make his or her self miserable. Even suicides love themselves; they just want to rid the self of suffering. Even self-hatred is self-love because, for whatever reason, it pleases you to think of yourself as a miserable, incompetent worm. I once told a friend, whose whole personality was centered around a deep sense of self-loathing, to get off his lazy ass, do his *karma yoga* and make his life beautiful. He said, "Well, my life may be shit, Jim, but it's warm and it's mine."

A clever Vedanta person may question the idea that both the lover and the beloved are the self because Vedanta repeatedly points out that the subject and the object are different. Saying that they are one seems to be a logical fallacy. But if something has different parts, from one standpoint it can be the subject and from a different standpoint it can be an object. If I touch one hand with the other, I am touching myself with myself. The self has a higher nature - pure, original, partless consciousness - and a reflected, lower, empirical nature that is manufactured by *Maya* solely out of its original nature. Therefore I can love my body/mind/sense complex as myself because it is not separate. At the same time, I enjoy freedom because I exist in an order of the reality that is free of my equipment and the world. *Isvara* talks about Its higher and lower "selves" in the *Bhagavad Gita* (4.6):

> "Though I am birthless and deathless and the Lord of all beings,
> I take birth again and again through my own *Maya* and then,
> after some time, I return to my original transcendental nature."

Creation evolves from the subtle to the gross. *Isvara* is so subtle that It is not subtle. But when *Maya* operates, *Isvara* assumes the role of Creator, without sacrificing Its original nature, and appears as a mini reflected *Jiva* endowed with a higher and lower nature and reduced powers of will, knowledge and action. Therefore "I love myself" means I love my own higher nature: existence-awareness-limitlessness. So non-dual devotion is not only possible, but every self-actualized person enjoys it.

Non-Duality and Duality Are Not Opposites

One might object, "If I sacrifice my dualistic point of view for the non-dual point of view and fail to achieve non-duality, I will wind up losing both." Or one might worry that since one doesn't know what it is like to experience non-dual devotion, it may not be as lovely as dualistic devotion, so it is better to stick with what one has than venture too far afield into non-dual devotion, given that non-duality and duality are opposed. To add fuel to the fire, Krishna stokes this fear when he says that non-dual devotion is difficult to attain:

> "The pursuit of the formless non-dual self is more difficult [than dualistic paths] because it requires non-attachment to the body [experience]. (*Bhagavad Gita,* 12:5)

Dualists are incapable of understanding that both an idea and its opposite can be true, although they are quite capable of believing that God and the Devil – which are thought to be opposing principles – exist together in reality. Non-duality is not opposite to duality, they are in different orders of reality. Non-dual awareness has been supporting the cosmic manifestation, which appears as a duality, forever. If non-dual awareness were opposed to the dualistic universe, the universe could never have existed. The very fact that the universe was created and sustained is evidence that awareness supports rather than opposes it. Thus non-duality exists in spite of duality and is the basis of duality. All self-actualized devotees have non-dual wisdom and still experience the dualistic cosmic manifestation. And not only is non-dual devotion not opposed to dualistic devotion, Vedanta says you can subject your mind to non-dual teachings and enjoy dualistic devotion.

Keep Your Duality

Raw grains and nuts become much tastier when they are roasted. Similarly, the fire of non-dual wisdom roasts and toasts dualistic devotion, making it tastier. Dualistic devotion is a stepping stone and only fructifies with the attainment of non-dual devotion. But when a non-dual devotee worships *Isvara,* it is an opportunity for enjoyment and mutual admiration. When the *jnani's jiva* meets *Isvara,* it is a celebration of a mutually successful relationship. The devotee appreciates the wonderful fact that *Isvara* has provided the scripture and the *guru,* and *Isvara* appreciates the devotee who has successfully walked to the top of the devotional staircase: *karma yoga, upasana yoga* and *jnana yoga*. Both revel in their freedom. Two non-demanding free beings enjoying each other is the best kind of relationship.

Isvara is weary of the demands and complaints of unevolved devotees. Any relationship that involves consistent demands will disintegrate. As the demands increase, the partners start to withdraw and the demands give way to dissatisfaction and conflict, and the relationship breaks down. The mathematics of demanding relationships is that when two halves join together for completeness, one half divides the other, resulting in one-fourth of a relationship, not a full relationship. Expectations are the essence of dualistic devotion, whereas non-dual devotion is expectation-free.

Duality Is the Basis of *Samsara*

Non-dual devotion makes dualistic devotion safer. Duality, secular or sacred, is the basis of *samsara.* The most salient characteristics of *samsara* are fear and desire. The *Upanishads* repeatedly declare that the cause of misery is duality expressing as separation between two people, between a person and the world or between a person and God.

The *Brihadaranyaka Upanishad* (1.4.2) says, "Certainly fear is born of duality." The *Taittiriya Upanishad* (2.7) says, "Even a little bit of difference is the source of fear."

Superimposing even a smidgen of duality – like the idea that "I depend on God" or "I am a small spark of God's Divine Fire" – generates fear.

Isvara is the cause of fear for a dualist because *Isvara* is the law of *karma,* which destroys and takes away undesirable and desirable things. In Chapter XI of the *Bhagavad Gita,* Arjuna, after an initial feeling of awe, became frightened when he realized that *Isvara* was "mighty time, the destroyer of wombs," meaning everything that is born. The *Katha Upanishad* (2.1.11) says, "Whoever sees duality will travel from death to death."

To purify the heart, dualistic devotion must be boiled in the fire of self-knowledge, just as we boil water to purify it. A non-dual teacher, Madhusudana Saraswati, has written many wonderful hymns in praise of Krishna, along with a classical non-dual text called *Advaita Siddhi,* which sufficiently resolves all logical objections raised by dualists. He says that if you mix non-dual and dualistic devotion, the result is more enjoyable than one or the other. Someone who understands that duality exists but is not real can intentionally "create" duality simply for the pleasure of indulging in various forms of devotional worship. With this understanding, the play of duality is even more joyful than non-duality. That is why all of our teachers enjoyed writing hymns of praise, in addition to Vedanta literature. Shaṅkaracharya himself wrote hymns of praise to all the deities, testifying to the fact that non-duality makes duality safer – less fearful – and more enjoyable.

15. "There are various definitions of the characteristics of devotion due to different points of view."

Narada defined devotion as reverential love directed toward the self. Although this love is non-dual, it expresses in various ways and is defined differently by different sages in *sutras* 16 through 19.

16. "Sage Vyasadeva says it is expressed and enjoyed by performances of ritual worship, etc."

This verse refers to the nine forms of devotion encapsulated in a famous verse from the *Bhagavata Purana* (7.5.23):

> "*Sravanam kirtanam vishnoho smaranam padasevanam archanam vandanam dasyam sakhyam atmanivedanam.*"

"*Sravanam*" means listening to the glories of *Isvara,* with and without attributes. "*Kirtanam*" means singing or talking about the glory of the Lord. "*Vishnoho*" refers to worship of God in any way, in any form or without attributes (i.e. pure awareness). "*Smaranam*" means constant remembrance. "*Padasevanam*" means serving in churches, temples, mosques and anywhere else. As Ramana Maharshi says in *Upadesa Saram* (verse 5):

> "Serving God in the form of space, air, fire, water, earth, sun, moon and living beings is true worship."

"*Archanam*" means speaking the Lord's name and offering flowers. "*Vandanam*" means prostrating mentally and physically before an image of the Lord. "*Dasyam*" is devotional service, which amounts to living a virtuous, non-injurious life in line with scriptural injunctions and prohibitions, which are *Isvara's* instructions. An ethical life is the greatest service to God. "*Sakhyam*" is cultivating a friendly relationship with the Lord. Finally, "*atmanivedanam*" is surrendering the "I-sense" and "my-sense" to the Lord, which is *karma yoga,* surrendering the results of all one's actions to *Isvara.* It is a contributing, not a complaining and controlling, attitude: "Thy will be done, O Lord." Surrender is all upside; you rest in awareness as awareness and lose all your anxieties at the same time.

Surrender is natural when you understand the non-dual nature of reality because the devotee is known to be *mithya,* an apparent devotee. And an apparent devotee is as good as a non-existent devotee. If the devotee is *mithya,* only God is left, and insofar as the devotee exists, he or she only exists as *Isvara.* Self-knowledge is simply the recognition that every experience is just the self loving the self.

17. "Spiritual discussion (*satsang*) is an expression of devotion."

In the previous *sutra, puja* and rituals are given prominence, which is relevant for energetic *rajasic* types who need to be occupied with something worthwhile instead of wasting time in gratuitous egoic pursuits. If you are not cursed with *rajas* and incline instead toward *tamas,* you needn't get blisters on your feet from lengthy pilgrimages; you can sit comfortably with a cup of tea and affectionately discuss the teachings with like-minded souls. You can enjoy video and audio *satsangs* on the Web.

18. "Shandilya says devotion is perpetual delight in the self."

When you know who you are, enjoyment of dualistic forms of devotion is like watching a play. On one level you may very well become emotionally involved, perhaps to the point of laughing or weeping, but when the curtain falls your emotions go back to normal, which shows that you never actually forgot who you were when you entered the theater; you just suspended that person for an hour or two. Similarly, when you practice dualistic devotion, you never lose sight of the fact that the joy you experience is the joy of your self.

At the beginning of my quest I worshiped Krishna, who I thought was someone else. I prayed to him for enlightenment. The other day, forty-five years later, my wife and I installed a wonderful Krishna icon in our living room which we worship every day. Because of the teachings, I now know that I am only honoring myself. Before and after non-dual knowledge you worship according to your *vasanas* because indulging them is just one of many forms of self-delight. The delight is perpetual because you are perpetual and your nature is *ananda,* love.

Non-Conforming Lifestyles Must Go

19. "Narada says devotion is expressed by sanctifying all activities and by intense anguish upon forgetting the Beloved."

Merely listening to *Isvara's* glory and doing *puja* is not enough; your lifestyle needs to reflect the simple *sattvic* purity of the self. Devotion without the purification of *rajasic* and *tamasic* tendencies and the habits they engender is useless. If you try to fit your spiritual practice into a busy extroverted life, your priorities are skewed. Your life should be centered around your practice, not the other way around.

The purpose of ninefold devotion is to turn the doer into a *karma yogi* and an inquirer because non-dual teachings prove that God is everything that exists. God appears as the five elements, and everything in the creation is a combination of them. Nothing belongs to you. Attachment is the desire to get or keep something. Therefore become a devotee and loosen your attachment and aversion to objects. As devotion increases, attachment decreases, even toward family members. "My" children are actually *Isvara's* children. I am a caretaker.

See to it that your relationships with others are straightforward and loving. The motto of the Salvation Army says, "How can you worship a God that you can't see when you are unable to worship people who you can see?" If everyone is *Isvara* and I am non-separate from *Isvara,* how can I treat others indifferently or rudely, much less hate them? If someone becomes a problem, remove yourself physically and let go of the relationship, but don't hate him or her, because to do so is only to hate yourself.

A pure devotee is free of attachment and aversion. Therefore when you perform any action, do it with a worshipful attitude. Parents whose whole lives are dedicated to their children often suffer when their children disrespect them. They should take the *Gita's* advice (2.38): "Regarding happiness and sorrow, gain and loss, victory and defeat as non-different prepares you for life. With this attitude you will not suffer."

My Relationship to Myself Is Not Incidental

Every object is of equal value, nothing is more important than anything else. If you see differences, you are not free. In this *sutra,* Narada expands our understanding of God from the particular to the universal. Moving from a myopic, self-centered view to a view that includes everyone and everything is the fruit of self-inquiry. All activities, including mundane tasks like brushing teeth, taking a bath or eating should be done as offerings to the Lord who dwells within the body. When I accept the results of my actions with an attitude of gratitude, events will not agitate me. Accepting results should be heartfelt, not mere lip service. *Karma yoga* is a deliberate discipline meant to correct the tendency to impulsively react to events. Hurt feelings, taking things for granted, violence and reactivity are signs that the devotee has forgotten the Lord. A beautiful verse says that for a devotee, "Miseries are not real miseries. Wealth is not real wealth. Forgetting the Lord is the real misery. Constant remembrance of the Lord is real wealth."

If you are a sincere devotee, you will experience anguish when you realize that you have forgotten to consecrate your actions, thoughts and feelings to the Lord. If you forget, you will gasp for the vision of *Isvara* like a fish out of water. You may forget close friends and family members, but such lapses are unimportant because these relationships are incidental, but my relationship to myself is not incidental. I cannot afford to forget who I am even for a moment, to be away from the bliss that I am even for a moment. *Karma yoga* is remembrance with every action.

20. "Devotion is correctly described in each of these ways."

The definitions of dualistic and non-dual devotion mentioned in the previous *sutras* are not contradictory.

21. "The Gopis of Vraja[16] are an example."

The ideal devotees described in the *Bhagavata Purana* passed through all three stages of devotion. Initially, they saw Krishna as a human form and enjoyed his company. Next, they saw him in everything they experienced. Finally, by associating with him they understood that Krishna was the self of everyone and everything. A famous verse in the *Bhagavatam* (10.31.4) says:

> "You are not actually the son of the Yasoda, O friend, but you are rather the indwelling witness in the hearts of all embodied beings. Because the creation needs you, you came to protect and enlighten us. We are not deceived by your human form. It is merely a costume created by *Maya*. You reside in our hearts and in the hearts of all beings."

So the Gopis enjoyed Krishna devotion, knowing full well that Krishna was not just another person and that their relationship with him was not a mere man-woman dalliance but a sacred communication between a devotee and *Isvara* in which each was intimately and intensely aware of the other's true identity. As there are no outward signs of this kind of relationship, it can only be understood with reference to the underlying motive, articulated in the next *sutra*.

[16]The *Bhagavata Purana* is a dualistic text from the devotion *darshana* that personifies the self as Krishna, an *avatar*, the self in human form. It is the story of his life on earth as a destroyer of evil, establisher of *dharma* and a teacher of self-knowledge. The characters and events in this thoroughly charming work are best considered from the perspective of the Vedanta *darshana*. As such they are beautiful symbols of many spiritual truths. Even though Krishna appears in the *Mahabharata*, the most popular *Purana*, as a teacher of *dharma* and non-duality, most Krishna devotees do not accept non-duality for various reasons.

22. "Even in the case of the Gopis, one cannot criticize them for forgetting the Lord's greatness."

Devotion stemming from desire or attachment born of lack of discrimination is improper, whereas devotion rooted in discrimination and knowledge is pure and beyond reproach. Indeed in the *Bhagavad Gita* (9.11) Krishna says that if a person doesn't know who he is, he will not treat others with love. Because reality is non-dual, everyone is non-different from you, so pure love is the only true basis for relationships.

23. "If you forget that every object [person] is consciousness [your self], only selfish passion remains."

Forgetting that objects are you is commonplace because objects don't appear as consciousness. We treat others as objects because *Maya* causes us to identify with the body/mind/sense complex and from that perspective otherness seems to be the truth, causing us to feel separate and incomplete. From this sense of otherness a desire to complete one's self through objects – mostly human relationships, but through various other avenues as well – arises. Desire is lonely, painful and blind to the needs of others.

24. "When you are motivated by selfishness, you are indifferent to the happiness of others."

Don't think that you will have time to love others only after you have attained non-dual love.

Loving others is the royal road to self-love. When your interest in others is only for the sake of what they can do for you, you will feel guilty because you are not fulfilling your bargain with *Isvara*. *Isvara* didn't bring you here solely for the purpose of getting what you want. You are expected to give as much as you take, preferably more. A person with non-dual vision would never dream of entering into a needy, self-centered, *adharmic* relationship, because *Isvara,* that ever-present, unchanging witness of your life, never approves of these relationships. To say that *Isvara* doesn't approve means that selfish relationships create a store of unconscious guilt that constantly leaks into the conscious mind and pollutes relationships. All the objects in the creation are stitched together with an invisible thread of consciousness and bound to each other by *Isvara's* love. It is the duty of everyone to love the objects that appear in one's life. In this way the harmony of the creation is maintained.

The last three verses – which are typical of the dualistic approach – present devotion as a personal emotional bonding with a particular symbol of the self. This approach has certain benefits, but a seeker of freedom should regard it as a temporary stepping stone to an intellectual appreciation of the Lord in all forms. Although informal dualistic devotion has certain benefits, it is basically attractive to *rajasic* and *tamasic* people and can easily degenerate into corrupt practices, known as *vamachara* devotion.[17] Personal worship – think "surrender" – offered to powerful spiritual and religious personalities and institutions – seems to inevitably lead to corruption, if the power, sex and money scandals that endlessly come to light in the spiritual world are any indication. Not only can it lead to corruption, but dualistic devotees usually waste years ignoring their issues and stagnating in duality, all the while thinking that they can indulge their worldly and spiritual tendencies and that the *guru* or a personal deity – often a dead saint – will ride to the rescue and confer liberation on them. Thinking that freedom comes without self-effort, disciplining the mind and self-inquiry, examining one's beliefs and opinions, is delusional.

Formal devotion – Vedanta – instills a deep appreciation of God in everything.

> "I am the taste in the water. I am the radiance in the moon and the sun. I am the *OM* in all the *Vedas*. I am the sound in space. I am the manliness in men. Moreover, I am the fragrance in earth. I am the heat in fire. I am the life in all beings and I am the austerity in ascetics." (*Gita*, 7-9)

Non-dual devotion is the basis of the practice of *karma yoga* and *upasana yoga*, which leads directly to liberation. As Ramana Maharshi says in *Upadesa Saram* (verse 5):

> "Serving the world with the attitude of serving the Lord is the true worship of God, who is the wielder of the eightfold forms: ether, fire, air, water, earth, sun, moon and living beings."

[17] This refers to the left-hand practices of the *tantric* doctrines, which involve ritualistic use of five heterodox items, including *madya* (wine), *mamsa* (meat), *matsya* (fish), *mudra* (parched grain) and *maithuna* (sexual intercourse).

What Isn't *Isvara*?

If someone asks, "What is God?" we reply, "What isn't God?" However, seeing God in everything is not the end of your spiritual story. To be free and to love yourself and others unconditionally, you need the devotion that is beyond all forms. You need to understand that you are the limitless self and that you are the love that creates, sustains and destroys the whole cosmos. With confidence you must say, as does Krishna in the *Gita* (10.20), "I am the self residing in the heart of all beings. I am the beginning, the middle and the end of all beings."

Non-dual devotion – constantly keeping in mind the oneness of all things – leads to God-love, which is self-love because God is non-different from myself.

Chapter II

The Glory *of the* Highest Devotion

CHAPTER II POINTS out that non-dual love is superior to *karma yoga* and self-inquiry. Nonetheless, since it cannot be attained without practicing *karma yoga* and self-inquiry, a devotee that tries to skip these essential means will not succeed.

25. "*Advaita* devotion is superior to *karma yoga* and *jnana yoga*."

Karma yoga and *jnana yoga* are paths or means, whereas self-knowledge is the destination. Between the means and the end, the end is always superior because we take to the means for the sake of the end, the unshakable conviction "I am limitless awareness" alone. The *Gita* (7.17-18) says that a wise person, someone exclusively engaged in devotional service, is superior to someone practicing self-inquiry.

A hungry person prefers to eat rather than sit and stare at his food. Undeniably, there is pleasure in anticipating a beautiful meal, but the greatest pleasure happens when you become one with your meal. There is no actual separation between *Jiva* and *Isvara*. Both are pure non-dual consciousness alone.

26. "After all, non-dual love is the fruit of all our endeavors."

Everything we do we do to satisfy ourselves. Complete self-satisfaction without recourse to objects is non-dual love.

> "The self-actualized person is greater than any ascetic and even greater than a *karma yogi*. Not only that, he or she is greater than the person who knows who he or she is but has yet to actualize self-knowledge. Therefore seek to actualize self-knowledge." (*Bhagavad Gita,* 6.46)

A self-actualized, as opposed to a self-realized, person enjoys an awareness that includes the perception of body, mind, senses and surroundings, but remains unidentified with them. The knowledge "I am limitless existence/

consciousness" has been fully assimilated because there is no sense of separation, and there is a palpable sense of satisfaction that expresses as love for everyone and everything, including the flawed ego. The non-dual devotee is free of object-love (and equally free to love objects) because non-dual unconditional love is its own fruit. This devotee is even greater than a noble person who knows intellectually that he is the self.

Humans are utilitarians: once something is no longer useful, we lose interest in it. A child doesn't give his beloved tricycle a second thought the moment his parents give him a bicycle for his birthday. When you get your first job, you immediately lose interest in your university. It is universally true that between the means – formal dualistic devotion – and the end, the end is always more valuable.

27. "Furthermore, the Lord dislikes the proud and is pleased with the humble."

On the surface, a proud person seems to think the world of himself, but pride is always compensation for a hidden sense of self-loathing. To say that the Lord "dislikes" pride seems to imply that the Lord is a person, since people are little more than their likes and dislikes. But the Lord is not a person. The verse means that there is conscious part of one's self (*Isvara*) that is hidden from the conscious mind but nonetheless impacts on it in various subtle and not-so-subtle ways. Recently a famous "non-dual" *guru* was forced to abandon his gurudom because pride in his enlightenment and, ironically, his false sense of moral rectitude caused him to abuse "his" devotees. If he thought about it at all, he probably justified the abuse with the idea that the end, the bliss of enlightenment, justified the means. Not only does this example speak to an erroneous notion of enlightenment – that someone else can discipline you to freedom – but it shows that some part of the self will work against you if you break reality's number-one law, non-injury. A humble person is a contented person. He knows that through the results of one's actions *Isvara* will see to it that narcissistic people are brought to book, and consequently keeps his head down. A wonderful verse in Handel's *Messiah* says that the Lord "makes the rough places plain." In the fullness of time even the mightiest mountains are reduced to plains.

Not only will *Isvara* correct your lifestyle if you are proud, it will make you suffer during your transgressions. Consistently doing what is wrong is tremendously enervating because you are forced to repress your true self, which will never break the rules, because it has nothing to gain by so doing. Additionally, maintaining the fiction that you are right when in fact you are dead wrong is completely debilitating. Furthermore, the self-loathing that your violations produce needs to be projected onto others because it contradicts your own good opinion of yourself. So while you may be feared or respected for some of your gifts, you are incapable of love and are never really loved, because you are an angry, unforgiving person.

If you were to ask God which devotee it likes the most, it would say:

> "Four types of virtuous people surrender to me: the distressed, spiritual materialists, seekers of knowledge and the wise. The one who is steadfast in non-duality is superior to the others. The others are certainly noble, but the wise person who has inquired into me with a steadfast mind has realized non-difference from me. He is me and I am him." (*Gita* 7.16-18)

And at the end of the twelfth chapter, Krishna describes the glory of such a wise person (12.14):

> "That devotee of mine whose mind and intellect are fixed upon me and who is ever-contented, tranquil, self-restrained and has clear knowledge of me is dear to me.

Summary

You love yourself completely when you know who you are. Non-dual devotion is the highest human achievement, a desireless, effortless "state" that requires no maintenance, because it is simply hard and fast knowledge of your fullness. A suffering devotee's attention is split between his problems and the self. A materialist's devotion is divided between desired objects and the self. Even the inquiring devotee is concerned about the departure date of his self-ignorance. They all want out of the world because they do not see the world as the self.

The discovery of one's ever-present innate fullness robs the non-dual devotee of motives. Fullness is freedom from desire, which is born of a sense of incompleteness and inadequacy. When you attain it, you love yourself completely because you are free of egoism. You are "a non-hater of all beings; friendly, compassionate, free from the 'I' and 'mine' notions, the same in comfortable and uncomfortable circumstances and indifferent to life's little miseries." (*Gita,* 12.13)

See the Mighty – How They Fall!

Narada is justified in saying that *Isvara* "dislikes" the egoic, possessive devotee because *Isvara* is the total mind, the collective consciousness, the universal rules that apply to everybody (*samanya dharma*). *Dharma* does not "like" ego, arrogance, tyranny, selfish desire, etc. Although their methods are often *adharmic,* revolutionaries and subversives are instruments of *Isvara* because they want to destroy tyranny, deceit, ignorance, possessiveness, etc. See the joy throughout the world when dictators invariably fall!

You may superficially think owning and possessing things is wonderful, but the feeling that you are trapped by them is *Isvara's* punishment for that belief. Subconsciously – *Isvara* again! – you know that you don't have a legitimate claim on anything, because it all belongs to *Isvara* insofar as *Isvara* creates, maintains and destroys everything. It was all here before we were born and it remains once we die. At best I am only a caretaker.

Swami Paramarthananda says, "The caretaker only has to take care; it is the owner's job to worry. Therefore if I become a caretaker and let *Isvara* be the owner, *Isvara* will handle the worry and I will be free of it. Every time worry affects me it means I have forgotten my caretaker status and I am claiming ownership. Ownership is taxing and will invariably be taxed."

Finally, *Isvara* considers the non-dual devotee wise and very dear because as long as a devotee thinks he is separate from *Isvara, Isvara* will not include him. *Isvara* is non-coercive and respects the devotee's right not to love himself or *Isvara. Isvara* is an impersonal part of the self that delivers the results of your actions. Thoughts are actions. So if you exclude *Isvara* from your thinking, *Isvara* delivers your *karma* in the form of the belief that you are separate from everything and incomplete in yourself. You may think *Isvara* is causing problems, but your refusal to accept *Isvara* is the problem. If you loved *Isvara,* you would accept everything as it is. *Isvara* is denied your love and your love denies *Isvara.* Don't, however, think that *Isvara* is waiting for your love, because *Isvara* is the source of all love and complete in itself, so it does not suffer when you refuse to love it. An individual that excludes anything from his or her love is not very intelligent. Whatever you resist persists. Non-dual devotees understand how futile it is to not love *Isvara* in the form of their thoughts and feelings and their life circumstances, so they gladly accept everything, including death. You love yourself when you accept yourself completely, both as *Isvara* – your body-mind and your life – and as the person you have been conditioned to think you are.

Otherwise you will be bedeviled by fear. The *Taittiriya Upanishad* says, "Even a little bit of difference is a source of fear," and the *Katha Upanishad* (2.1.11) says, "Whoever sees division or duality will travel from death to death."

How Do I Gain Non-Dual Devotion?

28. "Some say that knowledge is the means for developing devotion."

Some sages say that self-knowledge is the only means for non-dual devotion because we can only love something we know. If I ask you to love a gagagubai, you need to know to what I am referring before you can offer your love. Furthermore, you should feel that it is worth loving. Someone told a woman that she could only love her husband if she understood him, and the woman replied, "It is precisely because I know him that I don't love him." Knowledge can lead to love or it can lead to court. Love has two preconditions: you should know the object and you should know that the object is lovable.

Similarly, love of God, dual or non-dual, won't happen unless we know what God is. Ironically, many question the existence of God, yet crave love. Science is no help, and most people aren't interested in the views of a group of homeless Hindu sages living in caves in the Himalayas. However, until you get knowledge of ever-free original consciousness and reflected consciousness, yourself, there is no possibility of gaining pure non-dual love, because you are love. Finally, desire and action stem from knowledge: if you know how beautiful you are, you will do what it takes to realize it. Knowledge is the means for devotion.

Original and Reflected Consciousness

Reality is non-dual, original consciousness/awareness/bliss, i.e. love. But when *Maya* is operating it produces a reflecting medium called the Subtle Body. Pure original non-dual consciousness plus the Subtle Body is an individual (*jiva*), otherwise known as a person, or if you prefer religious terminology, a soul. Although pure ever-free consciousness never becomes an individual reflection, *Maya* makes it think it is a person. This confusion is called superimposition (*adhyasa*) and produces suffering, a sense of limitation that compels the soul to seek love in objects. Self-knowledge removes superimposition, which reveals the fact that the self is love, sets the reflection free of the belief that objects supply happiness and gives it the opportunity to love itself unconditionally because the reflection is non-separate from self. Even though you can't see your face with your eyes without the aid of a mirror, when you look into a mirror you don't see anyone else. Vedanta is the word mirror that proves you are love.

29. "Others say that devotion and knowledge are mutually interdependent as cause and effect."

Some sages contend that you cannot say that knowledge is the means and devotion is the end, because devotion is also a means. You need to love an object before you will invest your time getting to know it. Therefore knowledge is the cause of love and love is the cause of knowledge. They are mutually interdependent. Do you exercise because you are healthy or are you healthy because you exercise? The apparent reality is an interconnected whole in which no object is different from or superior to another.

30. "But Narada says that devotion is its own fruit."

By implication Narada seems to be saying that the means, dualistic devotion, will eventually become the end just a green banana becomes a yellow banana. If there is no connection between the means and end, Narada is a dualist, which is unlikely, because he was properly taught by a great sage. But Narada means that dualistic devotion qualifies the devotee for self-inquiry (i.e. *sravana, manana, nididhyasana*), which leads to self-knowledge, which in turn seemingly converts dualistic devotion to non-dual devotion.

Action Can't Produce Non-Dual Devotion

Dualists tend toward magical thinking. In the dualistic spiritual world, which tends to be aggressively knowledge-averse, there is a very common belief that by chanting the name of the Lord, for instance, the devotee will miraculously gain enlightenment or enter into some kind of transcendental state beyond the world. Apart from the fact that there is nothing beyond the world, because the world is non-dual existence/consciousness, Vedanta says that self-knowledge is compulsory. You can't skip it. "May you gain knowledge by prostration, service and proper inquiry. The wise sages will impart that knowledge to you." (*Gita* 4.34)

In the first place, chanting is an action done by a limited entity, a chanter. Any action done by a limited entity will not produce a limitless non-dual result, i.e. unconditional love. All results of actions, mental and physical, are limited, i.e. dualistic. Secondly, if self-knowledge happens automatically and effortlessly by chanting the Lord's name, there is no reason for the ancient and profound teaching tradition of Vedanta. Probably the best explanation for this belief is that people are lazy and some *gurus* need an easy way to make a living. They say, "Let us initiate you into a secret *mantra* and one day, by the grace of God, you will be free." It is not uncommon for Western seekers to pay through the nose for initiation into "secret" *mantras* that daily blare incessantly from tens of thousands of temples throughout India. The extreme wealth amassed by Maharishi Mahesh Yogi, of Transcendental Meditation fame and *guru* to The Beatles, was built primarily on this idea.

Praying, chanting and meditation will not produce self-knowledge. And if they do, the self-knowledge will disappear when the epiphany caused by the practice ends. Such activities are valuable for mental purification insofar as they build faith in non-duality, but since ignorance of one's self as limitless awareness is the actual problem and it is hardwired, only the consistent systematic practice of self-inquiry will establish hard and fast self-knowledge in the mind of the inquirer. Firm self-knowledge is liberation and liberation is non-dual devotion because there is only one self and its nature is pure love (*parama prema svarupa*). So the missing link between dualistic devotion and non-dual devotion in this verse is self-inquiry.

Self-Knowledge Cannot Produce Non-Dual Devotion Either

Contrary to a common belief in the non-dual world, self-knowledge does not produce non-dual wisdom/love, because non-duality is not a product of anything. It is the nature the self, existence/consciousness, which is prior to everything. It cannot be produced, reached, brought to birth, perfected or changed by any action. It is eternal and immortal. It does not convert dualistic devotion to non-dual devotion, although it seems to. It simply negates ignorance, the belief that duality is real. As we are told in the *Brihadaranyaka Upanishad* (2.4.14):

> "An object of knowledge is effortlessly known [assuming the means of knowledge are operating properly]. If there is something other than the eyes and the ears, the eyes can see it and the ears can hear it. The nose smells, but it does not smell itself. Only remote vibrations can be heard by the ears. The spoken word is a product of speech. Only if thoughts are different from their objects is thinking possible. Understanding too is possible only if the object to be understood is different from one's understanding."

The verse means that the dualistic devotion experienced at the beginning of one's quest is actually non-dual devotion because there are not two kinds of love: love is love. When you love an object you really love love because the object invokes the love that you are. If the love was in the object, the same object would give love to everyone, but this is not the way it is. Non-dual love looks like dualistic devotion because the devotee is ignorant of his true nature. If you build a wall in the center of a room, you have not actually divided space, because space pervades the wall as well as the room. If you knock the wall down, the space doesn't reappear, because it wasn't removed when you built the wall in the first place. The devotee does not become *Isvara,* the devotee is *Isvara* all along.

Bliss Is Love, Love Is Bliss and Hate Is Love

The self is existence, consciousness and bliss (*satchitananda*). These words do not refer to three aspects of the self; they are synonyms. When and where *Maya* operates, the limitless reservoir of potential "stored" bliss becomes experienced as love. Expressed bliss is love and stored love is bliss. When bliss, like a river, flows toward objects as love, it takes different forms. In *samsaris,* expressed love is tainted by ignorance – the belief that the object toward which it flows is a source of love – and becomes attachment. When the flow of love toward an object is obstructed, it is transformed into hate. As the *Bhagavad Gita* (3.37) says:

> "Love is desire. It is also anger transformed by *rajas*. It is insatiable and an inveterate sinner. In this form, know it to be an enemy of life."

Although a mother loves her child, she gets angry when the child does not follow her instructions. All negative emotions, jealousy, for instance, are flowing love. However polluted it becomes, water can be purified and made drinkable. When object-love is purified by self-knowledge it becomes compassion, empathy, affection and desireless devotion for God, a great moral power. We all have love because love is bliss and bliss is the nature of the self.

Dualistic devotion is motivated love; it is not pure love, which is motiveless. Dualistic devotees don't want the Lord, they want the Lord to give them some object. To extricate one's love from attraction to objects, one needs to convert one's emotions into devotion. In this way dualistic devotion "becomes" non-dual devotion. Love is the means and love is the end.

31. "For example, dinner in the palace of a king."

For uninformed people, devotion is only a means to an end. The idea that devotion is an end in itself is unknown to them. An invitation to dine with the President at the White House is a great honor in itself; hunger-removal is merely incidental. So a meal that's normally a means to an end becomes an end in itself. Similarly, devotion should become an end in itself. Self-love is self-validating. This is further explained in the next *sutra*.

32. "Just as a king is not satisfied by merely observing his palace from afar but lives in it, a hungry person is not satisfied by the mere sight of food."

Just as the President is not honored by my visit, *Isvara* is not going to feel honored by my devotion. *Isvara's* self-esteem is total. The President didn't invite me to remove my hunger. So even though hunger will be removed as a result of the meal, eating with the President is its own honor and accomplishment. Similarly, non-dual devotion should be pursued as its own end, not for any other purpose. Failure to understand this idea causes enlightenment sickness, using devotion to gain power, fame, pleasure, wealth and recognition.

33. "Therefore seekers of liberation should take to devotion."

The verse implies, but does not explicitly state, that seekers should take to Vedanta because the pursuit of self-knowledge is the highest form of dualistic devotion. It need not be stated, because educated inquirers are well aware of the role of self-knowledge with reference to non-dual devotion; it removes the obstacles to our appreciation of ourselves as love, since the self is love.

Seekers of freedom from attachment to objects – a perverted form of love – should seek non-dual devotion because it destroys attachment to objects. Loving God is loving myself and the world because God includes the world. Discovering my identity with *Isvara* means that, since *Isvara* has everything, I have everything already. Therefore I love what I have, not what I think I don't. Born of admiration, non-dual love is complete, unvarying, ungraded, universal love of my true original self, my created apparent self, the world and the Creator of the world. It is total confidence that nothing is missing. It is effortless and unquestioning self-esteem. It is not self-critical. There is no second-guessing; whatever the non-dual devotee does, he does without reservations.

Chapter III

The Means *for* Discovering Devotion

CHAPTER III PRESENTS the formal dualistic practices required for achieving unconditional love and emphasizes the value of values in the pursuit of liberation.

34. "Great teachers have declared means for achieving non-dual devotion."
Whereas the dualistic *darshana* contends that formal dualistic devotion is optional, Vedanta contends that informal dualistic devotion is optional and that formal devotion is mandatory. The reasons for this are explained in Badarayana's *Brahma Sutras*.

The following verse discusses formal dualistic devotion, a topic expounded in the seventh chapter of the *Gita,* which presents the four types of devotion enumerated above. The suffering devotee and the object-oriented devotee in each of us need to become an inquiring devotee to obtain God's grace: exposure to a qualified teacher of Vedanta and enthusiasm for *karma yoga* because it nourishes the desire for inquiry and turns the spark of desire for freedom into a raging fire. The *Vedantasara*[18] conveys the intensity of this desire (*mumukshutva*):

> "Just as a person whose hair is on fire immediately jumps into the nearest pond to quench the flames, a qualified student, scorched by the self-deluding flames of duality (*samsara*) eagerly rushes to serve a competent teacher, who having discovered his innate ever-free self, rests in uninterrupted serenity."

The desire for self-knowledge, the number-one means, should become so intense that an inquirer is eager to practice *karma yoga* and *upasana yoga.*

[18]*The Essence of Vedanta,* a 15th-century Vedantic text written by Sadananda Yogendra Saraswati.

These disciplines increase the desire for freedom and the capacity of the mind to receive self-knowledge.

Beauty, Variety and Novelty, but No Stability

35. "One gains devotion by giving up sense gratifications and associations with worldly objects."

A person is not qualified for inquiry until he or she has converted the desire for worldly happiness into a desire to know the truth. As long as there is the slightest belief that the world can supply peace, happiness and security, one should remain a seeker of objects and take the suffering without complaint. The world can supply beauty, variety, novelty and excitement, but it cannot supply stability. In fact it creates attachment to unstable things.

Less Is More

Worldly people's lives are cluttered with material objects and gratuitous activities. The *mantra* of an inquirer is "less is more." Less stuff and fewer trivial activities equals more peace of mind. A lovely verse in the *Mukundamala Stotra* says:

> "O Lord, I am not attached to spirituality, wealth or sense enjoyments. These things come and go according to my *karma*. I have one prayer and one prayer alone: from one moment to the next, may I render unflinching devotional service at your lotus feet."

You can simplify only up a point because certain things are necessary to sustain life. However, once the clutter is gone, drop your sense of ownership toward what remains and become a caretaker, knowing full well that everything belongs to the Lord. How is this accomplished?

A Simple Life Is a Simple State of Mind

Simplifying your life doesn't necessarily only mean removing material clutter or doing fewer activities. Your "life" is not objective; it is purely subjective. Nobody else sees it like you do. Your life is just how you think about your *karma*, your life situation. So simplifying means simplifying your state of mind by reducing complicated thinking. Trying to find a solution to a problem when you see that the problem and the solution are equal creates a very complicated thought process – dithering – which basically paralyzes you. If you are not doing everything you can to solve the problem, then you need to do appropriate actions, but if you are doing everything possible, then you simply need to accept that you are not intended to be the one that finds the solution and you leave the solution to *Isvara*. The solution will not come as long as you take responsibility for it. *Isvara* is non-coercive; it will not rob you of your free will. If you turn it over to *Isvara,* you put *Isvara* on the spot and *Isvara* will present a new set of circumstances that will lead you out of the problem.

36. "One achieves devotion by worshiping the Lord ceaselessly."

This means regular, uninterrupted devotional practice as prescribed in the scriptures. Krishna discusses these exercises throughout the *Gita*. For example, in verse 30 of the third chapter he says:

> "Offering all actions unto me with a devout mind, live without expectations, possessiveness and anxiety."

And in verse 10 of the fifth chapter:

> "Dedicating all actions to the Lord, the one who acts without attachment for the results is not affected by agitation, just as a lotus leaf is not made wet by water."

Verse 27 of the ninth chapter says:

> "Whatever you do, whatever you eat, whatever you offer as oblation to the sacrificial fire, whatever charity you give and whatever austerities you undertake, dedicate them as offerings to me."

And verse 58 of the eighteenth chapter:

> "With your mind fixed on me, you shall cross over all obstacles by my grace. But if you do not listen due to egoism, you will perish."

These practices boil down to the ninefold devotions unfolded in the commentary on verse 16.

Delusion concerning the nature of the self and the meaning of life is born of ignorance.

To remove ignorance, knowledge of *Isvara,* the cause, and the world (*jagat*), the effect, is necessary. The inquirer needs to determine which is more reliable. Vedanta says that the cause is reliable and the effect is unreliable. The cause is always available because it is always present, whereas effects come and go. The cause is one alone (*eka*), essential (*sara*), eternal (*nitya*) and true (*satya*), whereas the effect is dependent, multifarious, non-essential, fleeting and unreal (*mithya*). Effects like the body and the mind are dependent on the cause, but the cause – your self – requires no support.

For instance, if you grind a clay pot into small particles, you only lose the pot, not the clay. The clay, which can be reconstituted as another pot, is essential, and the pot, which cannot reconstitute itself, is non-essential. The clay is independent, the pot dependent. The clay is substantial (*satya*), the pot insubstantial (*mithya*). It has no existence apart from the clay. You, consciousness, are the clay, and your body-mind is the pot. The choice is a no-brainer if you want peace, security and happiness.

Depending on your state of mind, *Isvara's* worldly set-up can be helpful or detrimental. You can see it as an opportunity to gain a peaceful, secure and happy God-centered life or you can foolishly try to cobble together a world of your own, hoping that it will bring peace, security and happiness. You may derive a certain degree of security from a job, wealth or a loved one, but one day the job, money or loved one that promised to protect you will be gone because life is in *Isvara's* hands, not in the hands of *Isvara's* reflections, whereas *Isvara,* your self, which is love and the greatest security, never deserts you.

From the threefold perspective of the apparent reality we have only one cause-and-effect relationship: the connection between our original uncreated consciousness and our reflected personal selves. Devotion is our nature because we are completely dependent on *Isvara,* ever-free, unborn, original consciousness. It is a unique unlimited relationship because it obtains before, during and after every discrete experience, whereas relationships with other reflections – even parents and children – are definitely limited. Our relationship with our self is definitely the more reliable of the two. Therefore it should be stabilized and enhanced by devotional practice. From listening to scripture unfolded by a competent teacher, I nourish my devotion as I come to understand why I should cling to my fundamental relationship with God instead of incidental relationships with objects, people particularly.

The instruction here is not to abandon relationships – it is impossible, because life is relationships. The idea is to abandon the need for them. You can just as well worship a loved one as the self rather than as a person to lean on or a shoulder to cry on.

Nourishing the relationship with *Isvara* is similar to the way we nourish relationships with loved ones. When we feel close to another person, we look for opportunities to be in constant contact: phone chats, texts, emails, gift-giving and spending time together. Similarly, even if we have worldly *karma,* it can be sanctified. Whatever we do, whatever we eat, the charity we give or the austerities we practice should be done as an offering to the self.

One Inescapable Relationship

Imagine that every action is a flower and every performance of that action is offering the flower at the feet of the Lord. The results of one's actions keep on coming; life is the results of action as interpreted by *Isvara,* the *dharma* field. Every mosquito bite is a result of *karma*. But whatever happens I should see as a gift bestowed by God. A reverential attitude turns my life into a ceaseless devotional practice. Fundamentally, I am a devotee who momentarily dons the mother, father, brother, sister, friend, husband or wife costume. Life's roles come and go, but my role as a devotee is constant and inescapable.

Verse 36 cautions us to abandon egocentric devotion in favor of a motiveless, expectationless appreciation of the created glories of the Lord as indicated in the tenth chapter of the *Bhagavad Gita*. This chapter says that wherever you encounter something exceptional in life, you should appreciate it as one of God's many splendors. Even tiny microbes and lichens growing on rocks are wondrous. If at all you have a motive, let it be gracious and pure like the sentiment in this peace *mantra*:

> May all beings be prosperous and happy.
> May all beings be free from illness.
> May everyone appreciate only what is spiritually uplifting.
> May no one suffer and may peace prevail everywhere.

Constant desireless devotion wears away the depressing constraints of egoism, possessiveness and attachment to one's body, family and friends.

37. "One achieves devotion by hearing and talking about the Supreme Lord's special qualities, in every relationship."

Humans are social animals. Everything that comes to us, good and bad, comes through others: first our parents, then neighbors, teachers, friends, employers, etc. A person who is unable to share his or her innermost feelings will be unhappy. So don't hide your light under a bushel; in the inevitable social situations life presents, look for opportunities to create an atmosphere that glorifies the Lord.

> "Fixing the mind and senses on me, mutually sharing the knowledge about me and speaking of me, non-dual devotees are always contented and delighted." (*Bhagavad Gita,* 10.9)

A recent study revealed the sad fact that sixty-eight percent of human speech is gossip. Obviously, gossip – negative evaluations of others – is spiritually counterproductive even though people's veniality and wickedness is a juicy topic. Calumny, fault-finding, is condemned in scripture. It disturbs the mind because it is born out of ignorance of the fact that the world is a shining reflection of God's glory and that human beings are, as the poet says, "the roof and crown of things," cast in the image of God. Of course it is inappropriate to foist one's devotion for the Lord on others at all costs.

Keeping in mind that nothing is as tiresome as proselytizing and it only serves to create resentment, the *Bhagavad Gita* says, "let not the wise unsettle the minds of the ignorant," meaning worldly people who have no spiritual inclinations. However, there are individuals in every situation that have spiritual inclinations. Seek them out and look for opportunities to steer the conversation in a spiritual direction wherever possible. Speak of the strengths, virtues and accomplishments of others, keeping in mind that these virtues are manifestations of *Isvara* alone. Speaking well of others is equivalent to chanting the Lord's name. Stimulating and reinforcing inspiring comments is a practical form of worship in secular situations. But a devotee should always have compelling reasons to leave when it is clear that there is no opportunity to turn the conversation in the right direction.

38. "However, the primary method by which one develops devotion is association with great souls."

A "great soul" is not necessarily a fully self-actualized human, as these are very rare and only come into one's life when one's store of merit is exceptional. A great soul is any cultured person committed to higher values who is devoted to the Lord. By avoiding upsetting words and concepts, one can even communicate effectively with narrow-minded religious types who believe that their path is the only way to salvation.

The ninth verse of Shankaracharya's *Bhaja Govindam* says, "Keeping the company of those who listen to, reflect upon and assimilate the truth leads to non-attachment. Non-attachment leads to freedom from delusion. Freedom from delusion leads to steadiness of mind. Steadiness of mind leads to liberation."

In materialistic societies it is difficult to keep the mind pure. Swami Paramarthananda gives an interesting metaphor. He says, "It is like the soft tongue, which is required for speech, one of human beings' most necessary activities, trying to avoid being bitten among thirty-two hard teeth. Once in a while it does get bitten, which is quite painful, but it generally manages well. May you skillfully avoid being bitten by the materialistic mindset. Developing this skill requires the grace of the Lord; good friendship is a rare and great blessing, and the company of *mahatmas* is rarer still."

Association with materialists destroys devotion, association with cultured devotees imparts a momentary spiritual glow in the mind, and association with communicative self-actualized beings sets the mind free.

39. "Contact with great souls is rare, difficult to understand and infallible."

Even though *satsanga*[19] is great, it is difficult to attain, because although we are awash in a sea of self-proclaimed spiritual experts, wise people are very rare in this world. In this verse, Narada is referring to fully self-actualized, free human beings, not just cultured devotees or self-realized people. The glory of such associations is profound, incomprehensible, indescribable and nearly unfathomable. How can one describe the flavor of a ripe peach?

It will infallibly convert a worldly person into a devotee, an atheist into a theist, a suffering devotee into a positive seeker, a spiritual materialist into an inquirer, and an inquirer into a wise non-dual devotee. The lives of undiscriminating *rajasic* and *tamasic* materialists are full of failures, but a life transformed by association with a *mahatma* never fails. It is infallible.

Seeking great souls rarely, if ever, works. You need an exceptional store of merit. How can one attain such merit?

[19]*Sat* means "the truth, the self." *Sanga* means "association." So *satsanga* is discussion during which the only topic is the truth. Vedanta teaching is *satsanga*. The word is popular in the Neo-Advaita spiritual world, but has been twisted into an oaccasionally helpful but strange ritual.

40. "The association of great souls can be obtained, but only by the grace of the Lord."

Grace is not a happenstance phenomenon. It is earned by living an authentic life dedicated to an uncompromising pursuit of truth. As Shankaracharya says in verse 3 of *Vivekachudamani*:

> "Three blessings are rare, difficult to achieve and attained only by the grace of God: a human birth, the desire for liberation and association with a great sage."

A proper *mahatma* is a self-actualized individual steeped in the Vedic tradition. Non-*vedikas* are not considered to be *mahatmas,* because without knowledge of the Vedic tradition, they present the dualistic ideas common to Yoga and the devotional schools, which view dualistic devotion as both the means and the end and consider informal dualistic devotion to be a direct means of liberation. These schools are knowledge-averse and vehemently assert that Vedantic study is not required, even going so far as to say that Vedanta is an obstacle to liberation because they mistakenly believe that it is devoid of "heart," meaning feelings. Vedanta is not averse to feelings insofar as feelings and emotions are an essential aspect of existence. In fact this text informs us how to use our love – the only feeling that really counts – constructively. Vedanta's analysis of the emotional aspect of human existence is second to none.

The non-Vedic devotional schools tend to attract sincere, experience-oriented, morally upright, emotionally focused, overly sensitive, romantic people with questionable self-esteem, prone to magical thinking. To view life through a predominately emotional filter is a severe spiritual handicap. These days, every ordinary Tom, Dick and Harry with a third-rate epiphany under his or her spiritual belt is an expert on liberation and non-dual devotion. Therefore may you be blessed with an association with a wise person who follows the *Upanishadic* tradition because the effect of such an association is immeasurable.

Traditional *satsang* will lead a seeker to Vedanta inquiry, whereas non-traditional *satsang* keeps the seeker away from its disciplined approach. In traditional teaching the devotee becomes more and more committed to scripture, which leads to contemplation of Vedanta's identity *mantras.* There are so many erroneous concepts floating around the spiritual world today that a devotee must learn how to differentiate between genuine and disingenuous ideas. Although difficult to develop, Vedanta encourages critical thinking. This is why the verse says that association with great souls, who are critical and often provocative thinkers, is difficult to achieve.

Because seekers live in spiritual twilight, it is difficult to tell who is a real *mahatma* and who isn't. A person whose teaching is a personal evaluation of his spiritual experiences, incidental views abstracted from associations with non-*mahatmas* and uncritical interpretations of spiritual books, is perhaps qualified to share but not to teach. Teaching transfers to the student a systematic methodology capable of removing ignorance. Because seekers are unclear about the nature of liberation, they don't know how to seek. If they knew what enlightenment was, they wouldn't be seeking in the first place, so they are generally incapable of determining whether or not a teacher is the real thing. In the land of the blind the one-eyed man is king.

The only way out of this predicament is prayer. Verse 3 of *Vivekachudamani* says, "These three blessings are rare, difficult to achieve and attained only by the grace of God: a human birth, the desire for liberation and association with a great sage." Seeking is a catch-22: association with great souls confers grace, but we are only led to great souls by grace. Therefore all we can do is pray.

41. "There is no difference between the Lord's grace and the great souls that manifest it."

How can we lump the grace of *Isvara* and the grace of *mahatmas* together? Because *mahatmas* have the firm knowledge that *Isvara* is their very essence. Even *mahatmas* who have dualistic devotion invoke *Isvara* at all times. If you worship such a *mahatma*, the worship goes on to *Isvara*; it never remains with the teacher. A person who asks you to "surrender" to him or her is a charlatan, not a genuine *mahatma*, someone who is surrendered to the teaching tradition.

As Krishna says, "Fixing the mind and senses on me, mutually sharing the knowledge about me and speaking of me, they are always contented and delighted." (*Gita*, 10.9) And, "He who does works for me, who is my devotee, who keeps me as the supreme goal, who is free from attachment and who is free from hatred toward all reaches me." (*Gita*, 11.55)

Teachers whose teachings change over time are not qualified teachers. The self doesn't change, and the means of realizing the self hasn't changed for thousands of years, so why should a teaching change? Individuals whose charisma is due to a particular epiphany on a certain path will collect followers, become attached to the idea of gurudom, teach what worked for them until their "devotees" become dissatisfied and start leaving for other *gurus*. Whereupon, desperate to retain them, they will dig up a "new" path, often some esoteric Tibetan teaching, and tout it as more "advanced" to keep their *satsang* alive. A proper teacher is eager to get rid of the disciple – for the right reason.

42. "Strive only for God's grace. Strive only for God's grace."

Sometimes, particularly in the West, seekers don't even know that *mahatmas* exist, much less what they are. However, considering the fact that you have to start somewhere, you should take whatever teacher and teaching comes your way without abandoning common sense. However, if a teacher says that God doesn't exist and/or has no devotion for God, as do most modern non-dualists, be very careful.

Because God has a bad reputation these days among spiritual types, owing to the misery inflicted on the world in Its name, unfulfilled individuals with strong spiritual *vasanas* are often tempted to assume a godlike role in the lives of equally unfulfilled seekers. This, coupled with the idea that freedom is freedom from the constraints of *dharma*, is an invitation to disaster. Even religious types who profess devotion to God are perfectly capable of misleading a devotee, not to mention abusing them in predictable ways. So if you must have a teacher, inoculate yourself with a sense of high self-esteem and surrender only to God in the form of common sense and reason, and take to *satsang*. Shankaracharya emphasizes this idea in verse 9 of *Bhaja Govindam*:

> "Non-attachment comes from association with wise and virtuous souls (*satsanga*), and freedom from delusion arises from non-attachment. Steady devotion arises when the mind is no longer deluded, and liberation in this life (*jivanmukti*) is the result of steady devotion."

43. "By all means, renounce all relationships with ignorant, negative, self-centered individuals."

The verse does not imply hatred of bad people, because God is in everyone. Instead, keep your distance and pray, "May the wicked realize their goodness, may the good attain peace, may the peaceful attain liberation and may the liberated help to set others free." Nobody sets out to be ignorant, self-centered and evil; but some are helplessly compelled by negative *vasanas* and bad environments.

Bad people doesn't mean criminals in this context, although it goes without saying that associating with criminals is foolish even for worldly people. It means cynical, atheistic whiners and complainers of all ilk. Many perfectly honest, respectable people feel hard done by and carry negative auras wherever they go. Associating with them only pollutes the heart. A devotee should minimize contact with materialists, particularly atheists. Atheists are often intelligent and can sometimes produce arguments that appeal to the skeptical part of one's self. And the definition of "bad" people should include morally good but self-deluded teachers.

In our tradition, atheism is called *carvaka,*[20] which comes from *caru,* which means "attractive," and *vak,* which means "speech." Such people will say, "Why worry about good and bad? Observe the world: good people get the short end of the stick and bad people prosper. Be practical." When suffering piles up, the mind begins to question whether or not God is compassionate. Therefore the first condition for *satsang* is to keep company with those who have faith in God.

The second condition is respect for *dharma* even though it is not always easy to determine which action is right and which is wrong, because reality is shades of gray. Thirdly, inquirers should value the Vedic tradition because the Sanatana Dharma, which includes both the texts on *dharma* and liberation, has completely worked out the knowledge of existence and can resolve any existential doubt in light of the non-dual nature of reality. To get answers, a devotee must thoughtfully and systematically analyze the scriptures.

If you have devotion for *Isvara, Isvara* will terminate relationships with morally corrupt teachers, self-deluded teachers and reasonably harmless teachers who "teach" their own experience. Talking about liberation does not remove one's ignorance of who one is. Even if it is initially inspiring and creates desire for freedom, it is ultimately frustrating because teachers who talk about the self and their enlightenment cannot impart the greatest gift to the devotee: a systematic method for removing ignorance. Indirect knowledge is not useless, but the self is not an object of knowledge, so a teacher needs a complete teaching that involves teaching by implication and reason if direct knowledge is going to produce non-dual devotion. In fact direct

[20]Carvaka *darshanam* is one of the heterodox schools of Indian philosophy, which rejects spirit and emphasizes materialism and philosophical skepticism.

knowledge is non-dual devotion. Vedanta is the end of the road spiritually, the "knowledge that ends the quest to know (who you are)." Nearly everyone *Isvara* brings to Vedanta has "studied" with many teachers. If the devotee understands the value of a proven means of knowledge and the need for a qualified teacher, he or she will not seek elsewhere. In fact your seeking ends when you surrender to Vedanta because the teaching makes it very clear who you are. From that point on, the work only involves removing obstacles to your appreciation of your non-dual self.

44. "Association with materialists causes anger, confusion, forgetfulness, loss of intelligence and total spiritual calamity."

Tell me who your friends are and I will tell you who you are. Although you can do both simultaneously, if there is any doubt, first get rid of negative relationships and then cultivate positive relationships. If you try to have your cake and eat it too, you will only end up with a conflicted mind.

If you don't get rid of negative relationships, you will devolve because ignorant materialists only value security and pleasure, not freedom, which they believe is not empirically verifiable and definitely not profitable. Associating when them fertilizes selfish impulses. As the *Bhagavad Gita* says:

> "When you dwell on the sense objects, a fancy toward them arises. From fantasies desire is born. Desire causes anger, and anger causes delusion. The deluded lose sight of their purpose. When you forget your purpose, you cannot discriminate. Without discrimination, your soul is lost." (2.62-63)

Self-centered consumers of material goods and frivolous experiences are not interested in scripture and *satsang*. My teacher, Swami Chinmayananda, said, "There are animal-men, men-men and God-men. Humans are men-men and can evolve into God-men or devolve into animal-men. Indulging in worldly *vasanas* converts a man-man into an animal-man."

45. "Rising like waves from association with objects, these bad effects amass into a great ocean of misery."

Rajasic and *tamasic* tendencies (*vasanas*) are a hidden cancer that are often only discovered when it is nearly too late to do anything about them. For example, you may think you are a very congenial person, but in certain circumstances you cannot control your anger. Or you may think that you have your drinking under control, when in fact you are an alcoholic. You may have a full-blown case of enlightenment sickness, yet think you are the humblest person. Negative tendencies start as tiny ripples but can gradually grow into a huge tsunami that will eventually shatter your mind. Nip desire in the bud before you have a chance to act it out. Initially, you may only think an object is nice, but nice quickly becomes an attraction, and an attraction becomes a value. When you value something, you want it. And when you get a taste of it, you want it more. The more you want it the more unattainable it seems and the more your self-esteem suffers; you feel like a failure because you are unable to control it at will. When your self-esteem suffers, you begin the long slide down the slippery slope of obsession, addiction and, ultimately, life-destroying depression, particularly if you try to treat your depression with chemicals. You may come to feel that your very "survival" depends on the object. There was an article in the paper today that said that a man lost his life savings – $780,000 – to two psychics who promised to reunite him with a woman he once loved.

At the first sign of desire, make a determination (*sankalpa*) not to pursue it and intensify your inquiry. "A stitch in time saves nine." Stay away from unspiritual people, including grandiose, narcissistic spiritual teachers who do not follow *dharma*. Period.

46. "Who crosses beyond *Maya*? Who crosses beyond *Maya*? Only the one who abandons material associations, serves the sages and becomes selfless."

Maya, the cause of *samsara,* the belief that reality is a duality and that the objects contain joy, is a beautifully intelligent force, a powerful temptress who makes the world seem attractive and exciting. In the *Gita,* Krishna, the self, warns: "This divine *Maya* of mine, consisting of three *gunas,* is indeed difficult to fathom. Only those who surrender to me cross over." (7:14)

1. Keep an eye on your relationships. If your friends prefer to shop and gossip, work relentlessly or party hearty and nary a word of God escapes their lips, it's time to find new ones. Associate with either wise devotees or committed inquirers.

2. Stay away from religious and spiritual people who use self-inquiry to further their ambitions. Some who are insufficiently committed to *moksa* – psychologists, life coaches and helpers in general – often use Vedanta to get ideas that will improve their careers, which is an improper use of spirituality. While it is not the kiss of death, it is better to use God to develop fortitude in the face of worldly difficulties. Spirituality is a noble-minded pursuit meant

for obtaining the qualifications for liberation, not for making the world work. The world works nicely when you are a dispassionate, discriminating, forbearing, devoted person.

3. Reduce your sense of ownership and authorship by handing over every object to God. See yourself as a caretaker, not a possessor. To reduce possessiveness, consciously train yourself to see the self in everything.

Your *karma,* which is facilitated by God, enters you into a contractual relationship with God, whether you like it or not. Checking into a body here is like checking into a motel. God gives you the equipment and the circumstances to work out your *karma,* but when your lease expires, you have to give it all back. An old proverb says, "Cattle, wife, children and home are the result of previous birth bondage. Once the debt is annihilated there is no relationship, and hence the end of suffering in this *samsara.*" Your wife and children are actually *Isvara's* wife and children. While this may be a disturbing fact, it is a fact nonetheless. Use devotion to give up attachments, not to get worldly things. The *Gita* says, "Renounce all actions and seek refuge in me, the non-dual reality. I will liberate you from all sins. Don't worry." (*Gita,* 18:66)

47. "Who goes beyond *Maya*? The one who avoids society, loves solitude, lets go of the belief that there is security in worldly situations and transcends the *gunas*."

Get away from everyday rituals and objects like smartphones and television. Society's conversion of luxuries into necessities has turned modern life into a fancy prison. It is not uncommon for a middle-class home to sport three TVs. We worry ceaselessly about weapons of mass destruction as we slowly die at the hands of weapons of mass distraction too numerous to mention.

Sometimes I am asked to recommend a spiritual practice. When appropriate, I occasionally recommend a media fast, yet to date no one has followed my advice. If you are incapable of enjoying your own company, you need a bit of work. If you want to progress spiritually, the following secret *mantra* should be chanted at all times: "Less is more." In case it is an inscrutable *koan* for you, it means "less busywork, including thinking and talking, is more peace of mind."

See if you can't appreciate this fact: you are always alone, even when you are with others. There is only one of us. We live in consciousness as consciousness. Thinking you are separate causes you to long for company. When you are with an apparent someone else, you are only with the thought of that person in your mind. They are never "out there" in the body they seem to inhabit. They are in you. And the thought of them is manufactured out of you, pure love itself. So when you love an object, you are only loving yourself. When you long for a companion, you are only longing to know yourself. Why belong to a group when you can belong to yourself, a blissful club of one with no membership fees?

Teach yourself to love your own company in the form of the reflected glory of silent awareness. Cultivate silence. We distract ourselves because our thought life is so messy and unfulfilling. The mind of a *samsari* is like a garbage can filled with society's gadget-filled detritus. Dare to confront the thoughts that the silence reveals. Pick through them and discard those that don't point to truth, and with the help of Vedanta organize the ones that do into a lovely bouquet of non-dual meaning.

Attachments do not break themselves; they have to be broken. The grand gesture – dropping out and running off to India – is not the way to go. You will be back soon enough, your spiritual tail tucked neatly between your legs. Work on them little by little. Of course you can pray to *Isvara* to remove them, but unless you actually put forth some effort, how can *Isvara* change your *karma,* insofar as *Isvara* is not a big controlling parent situated somewhere else? It is just a mechanism in you that facilitates your *karma.* Grace, contrary to popular opinion, is earned.

Growth, including spiritual growth, involves a certain amount of pain. A *tamasic* mind will resist when you stand up to your desires and refuse to indulge your fears.

Creating a sense of simple self-reliance is not really difficult when you honestly consider the downside of relationships. Nothing lasts. Where are all those people now who once professed eternal love to you? As their minds changed, they moved on and pursued other relationships in search of meaning. *Isvara* is not only that part of you that facilitates your choices, it is the part of you that wants to be free – because it is eternally free. If you cooperate with that part by following the advice of the sages, who are non-separate from *Isvara, Isvara* will cooperate with you. There is no doubt about it. Standing alone in silence does not mean – once you have weaned yourself of the need for relationships and enjoy yourself alone – that you are condemned to a lonely life. Far from it. When you are self-reliant, you are very attractive, so people want to be with you. But once you appreciate your ever-present aloneness, you can mingle with others without attachment. Renunciation does not mean freedom from objects – relationships are objects – it means freedom from attachment to objects. When you love people because you need them, you are not free. When you no longer need them, you are free to love them for who they are.

Narada's final instruction in this verse is: wean yourself away from all desires except the desire for freedom. Spiritual growth is a sublimation psychology. You cannot just get rid of your desires for worldly things in one go. The desire for objects needs to be patiently redirected into the desire to know the truth of your non-dual nature.

Narada's final instruction is borrowed from one of the *Gita's* most important verses (2.45), which is the basis of *karma yoga*:

> "The *Vedas* deal with the world of the three *gunas*. Be free of *rajas* (passion) and ignorance (*tamas*). Be always established in mindfulness (*sattva*). Be free from the pairs of opposites. Be free from the desire to acquire and protect."

The word "*Vedas*" in this quotation means the portion of the *Vedas* that is concerned with how to live in the world. The *gunas* are material energies that bind individuals to the world. Two, *rajas* and *tamas,* are unhelpful, and the other, *sattva,* is helpful. *Tamas* (*avarana shakti*) hides the unreal nature of objects from us, allowing *rajas* (*vikeshepa shakti*) to create passion for them. *Sattva,* the revealing power of *Maya,* allows us to see things clearly and therefore to discriminate wisely.

The original rendition of this verse introduces two technical Sanskrit words, *nistraigunya* and *niryogaksema. Karma yoga* is one of *Isvara's* laws and is useful for (1) *samsaris* who want to remove stress to enhance their pursuit of objects but have no interest in *moksa,* and (2) for *karma yogis* who follow the action portion of the *Vedas* as a preparation for self-inquiry. *Karma yogis* are trying to free themselves of the *gunas*, hence the word "*nis*" (not) *traigunya.*

"*Niryogaksema*" is another interesting revealing word that refers to the need to expand our base in terms of family, possessions, money, status, recognition, etc. Fair enough, but getting things (*yoga*) enjoys an obvious and more difficult downside: keeping them (*ksema*). Losing weight, for instance, is a herculean effort to say the least, but keeping it off is even more difficult. When you enter into a relationship, particularly a "love" relationship, you feel remarkably happy, but a relationship's constant companion, fear of loss, comes with it. As long as acquisition/loss-anxiety crowds the mind, there is no room for *sravana, manana* and *nididhyasana*. The bottom line: don't focus your attention on securing your future. Abandoning objects does not mean physical abandonment but letting go of attachment to the "pairs of opposites," the likes and dislikes the mind associates with objects.

The *Bhagavad Gita* says, "Someone who neither hates nor desires, who is beyond the pairs of opposites, is effortlessly freed of bondage." Lest you give in to worry about worldly things when you commit to letting them go, the *Gita* gives an assurance: "With a heart that knows no otherness, steadily keep your mind on me [the self] alone and I will take care of your getting and keeping."

Worry is unnecessary, because the results of your actions are out of your hands. If you are facing a difficult patch, *Isvara* will give you the strength to handle whatever life throws your way. The best life insurance is devotion, surrender at the *karma yoga* level.

Life Is a Zero-Sum Game

48. "Who is capable of crossing *Maya*? The one who transcends the pairs of opposites and renounces the materialistic point of view."

The materialistic point of view boils down to the idea that objects are a source of joy, not the self. Duality may seem like an abstract concept, but it operates in our minds all the time in the form of "the pairs of opposites." The pairs of opposites are attractions and aversions, our likes and dislikes. Where there is attachment to joy, there is aversion to sorrow. Attachment to gain is always accompanied by avoidance of loss. The verse says that you should see that an attraction is just an aversion with a different name and vice versa. Experiences are generated by *Isvara* – who is not a big *Jiva* with likes and dislikes – according to the individual's *karma*; they are value-neutral. *Isvara* sees everyone and everything equally. The *Bhagavad Gita* (9:12) puts these words in *Isvara's* mouth: "I am the same toward all beings. No one is hateful or dear to me."

So the fundamental devotional practice is *karma yoga*. Whatever happens is the result of previous choices. Since we have no choice concerning the results of those choices, we need to learn how to accept what happens without resistance, reactivity and rejoicing. *Karma yoga* is seeing *Isvara* in every experience, a stepping stone to seeing everything as *Isvara* itself. Whatever comes will go. "Regarding happiness and sorrow, gain and loss, victory and defeat alike, prepare for the battle of life. In this manner, you will incur no sin." (*Gita* 2:38)

Karma yoga is not only right attitude, it is right action. Actions are classified in terms of how well they serve to prepare the mind for inquiry. They are (1) *sattvic*, those that give maximum spiritual benefit, (2) *rajasic*, those that are neither beneficial nor detrimental, and (3) *tamasic*, those that are harmful and lead one away from the goal.

The third class of actions, *adharmic karmas*, are not recommended for anyone and are definitely prohibited for a *karma yogi*. Although they may bring a particular physical or psychological gain to the doer, they harm the animate and inanimate objects in the *dharma* field and bring the doer down spiritually. They are to be avoided at all costs. The second class of actions are not necessarily *adharmic*. They do not involve injury, except inadvertently, to oneself or others, but are self-centered, compelling the doer to ignore the needs of others. They don't bring spiritual benefit – or very little, perhaps – nor are they necessarily detrimental, but they are directed toward material ends.

The first class of actions, *sattvika karmas*, are necessary if *karma yoga* is going to bear fruit. They are giving *karmas*, not grabbing *karmas*. The more you give, the more you grow. Your likes and dislikes are created by a grasping attitude. Without putting too fine a point on it, they are undone when the opposite attitude is in play. *Karma yoga* involves actions that add value to every situation, offerings that contribute to the well-being of the *dharma* field. The intention of a *karma yogi* is to enshrine *sattvic karmas* at the forefront of his or her life, to see that *rajasic karmas* are relegated to subordinate status and to eliminate *tamasic karmas*. Of course it is impossible to eliminate *tamasic* actions altogether. Certain unavoidable situations will cause the doer to injure herself or others. One should always strive to do *sattvic karmas* because they bring about maturity and spiritual growth by neutralizing the agitation that is born from the inevitable contact with unholy situations and people.

Karma Yoga and Sins of Omission

"Sin" is an archery term that means "to miss the mark." Sins are self-insulting actions that bring disrepute to the "sinner," the self under the spell of *Maya*. They are of two types: sins of commission and sins of omission. Sins of commission are actions that run contrary to *dharma*. They injure one's self and others. The most obvious emotion associated with sin is guilt. Sins of omission do not arise from our *vasanas*, but they produce unhelpful emotions that arise from the failure to do what is required in a given situation, the most common example of which is failure to pay taxes.

The Five Offerings

The "five offerings" (*pancha maha yajnas*) are compulsory actions not born of our likes and dislikes that are required for the formal *karma yoga* practice, the omission of which results in bad *karma* (*papa*). Bad *karma* is experienced as subjective turmoil; it prevents the flow of love to the people in one's environment and prevents inquiry.

1. Worship God in any form. One of the biggest problems with the Western non-duality world is disdain for religion, which is understandable from a certain point of view, insofar as unbelievable suffering has been inflicted in its name. But to abandon the religious impulse, which is just the self loving itself, because the church loses sight of the religious spirit from time to time, is foolish. The need to worship God is as hardwired as the desire for an identity. *Karma yogis* worship *Isvara* by surrendering the results of their actions to *Isvara,* trusting that *Isvara* knows what's best.

2. Reverence for parents. Most of our stuff, positive and negative, comes from our parents. You can't blame them, because they picked up what they handed to you from their parents when they were too young to think for themselves, although you have to look into it. As long as there is no resentment toward your parents, as long as you can see that they did their best according to what they knew and if you can see the gifts they did give and honor them in your thoughts daily, this is enough.

3. Worship of scriptures. The purpose of *karma yoga* is to gain a contemplative disposition so that you can assimilate the meaning of the teachings. But you should not think that you will start inquiry one fine day when you are contemplative. You should set aside half an hour or an hour a day or more for study of Vedanta. You don't become contemplative all at once. You have contemplative moments throughout the day and insights all along. The progression from an outward-turned mind to an inward-turned mind is gradual. One day you will realize how clear and peaceful your mind has become, even in the midst of a busy life. *Karma yoga* is for doers who have a strong desire for freedom and who understand the value of knowledge.

4. Service to humanity. When someone wants something from you, see if you can't give them what they want, assuming it is a reasonable desire. If you are helping others, at least you are not wasting your time indulging *tamasic* and *rajasic* habits. Service work cultivates *sattva.* It is difficult to practice, because the ego can easily imagine that it is superior to those who only look after themselves. So it is important to keep it simple – avoid grandiose "save the world" ideas. There are usually motivated by the desire for fame. *Isvara* presents opportunities every day to serve others. Service doesn't just mean doing what others want you to do, although it may. It means being open to others, not shutting them out. Serving others requires considerable mindfulness because ego, born of a sense of inadequacy and inferiority, looks for opportunities to feel special and virtuous. Service to others should be based on a recognition of the essential oneness of all of us. It is also wise because everything we need comes through others. Service-oriented individuals are generally well looked after.

5. Worship of all sentient beings. The appreciation of the oneness of everything should include all life forms. Practice it by respecting the environment. Recycle. Be conscious of your carbon footprint. Go green. Vegetarianism is a good way to worship life.

The essence of *karma yoga* worship is renunciation of the results of actions. It is a difficult practice, because we perform actions precisely for the results. If you are asked to renounce the results, why would you perform any actions at all? The answer is twofold: (1) action is not optional; insofar as I am alive, I am helplessly impelled to act by the three *gunas,* and (2) I want to be worry-free so that my mind is available for self-inquiry.

Compulsory actions produce material benefits, such as money, name, fame, status, possessions, etc. and also spiritual benefits: a mind qualified to understand non-duality, a proper teacher and the opportunity to study scripture. Unfortunately, we can only choose one or the other, not both, because the results are mutually exclusive.

Non-performance of the five contributions produces the sin of omission. Not doing them prevents *moksa* and the realization of non-dual love, which is an unwanted benefit for a seeker. If you are committed to *moksa,* non-dual love, there is no choice; you will be uninterested in the material benefits and gladly accept the spiritual benefits which come by default, if the material benefits are rejected. Spiritual results are called good *karma* (*punya*) and are experienced in the form of peace of mind and high self-esteem. When you do what's best for your spiritual side, you feel very good about yourself. Conversely, when you go for the material benefits, you are weighed down with worries. So a *karma yogi* doesn't fail to make the required contributions to the *dharma* field, but makes them with a deliberate intention to eventually become free of *samsara* and love everything as he or she loves the self.

Karma yoga necessarily involves a change in lifestyle. We need not drop out and head for a cave, but should gradually reduce worldly activities and self-inquire. *Karma yoga* can be totally given up when one gives up the householder's life. But *karma yoga* as knowledge can't be given up, because it is virtually the same as *jnana yoga*, the understanding that the self is not a doer. Self-actualized individuals act spontaneously in the *karma yoga* spirit, not as a conscious discipline.

49. "Who is capable of transcending *Maya*? The one who renounces even the *Vedas* and obtains exclusive and unbroken love of God."

Even though someone lives the life of a householder, he is a renunciant if he is dispassionate toward everything. This type is defined in the *Bhagavad Gita*, Chapter V, verse 3: "One who does not desire or hate is a *sannyasi* by temperament. Such individuals are effortlessly free of duality." Effortlessly means that the *karma yoga* discipline is not necessary, because this person is free of likes and dislikes. It does not mean that he is automatically self-actualized, only that he has no doubt about who he is and therefore does not require Vedanta (the *Vedas*) anymore. Once the knowledge has been gained, the means becomes irrelevant. As Shankaracharya says in *Nirvana Dasakam* (verse 7):

> "There is no ruler nor rule; no pupil nor training; no you nor I. This universe is not real, for the realization of the true nature of the self does not tolerate any distinction. That one, the residue, the auspicious, the alone, am I."

His is a life of assimilated self-knowledge, and from that point on unbroken self-love obtains. The wise person enjoys the causeless and abiding joy born of self-knowledge. Does this wise person derive joy from the reflected self or from the universal self? This distinction is rendered irrelevant because self-knowledge destroys the idea that they are different. In essence, what is the difference between a ray of sunlight and the sun itself? If there is only one self, it is limitless and therefore full. The fullness of one's self is non-dual love. The *Bhagavad Gita* (3.17) again: "However, there is nothing more to be accomplished for the one who loves the self alone, is happy with the self alone and who is contented with the self alone."

And the *Mundaka Upanishad* (3.1.4) says, "With every breath, the self-actualized person effortlessly observes the indwelling self, which is non-separate from the self in everything." A verse in the *Yoga Sastra* says, "A wise person sees no difference between a nugget of gold and the excreta of a crow." And Chapter VI, verse 29 of the *Bhagavad Gita* says, "One whose mind is disciplined through inquiry perceives the self in all beings and all beings in the self. He values everything equally."

It bears repeating that the many heterodox non-*advaitic* devotional schools don't see it this way, because they appeal to *tamasic* individuals who dislike discipline. They devalue *karma yoga,* the five contributions and Vedantic inquiry, and are happy to renounce them before they even practice them. They argue that you need only love *Isvara,* which they prefer to call *Bhagavan,* morning, noon and night, and one fine day he will appear to whisk you off to *moksa*. But renunciation of the *Vedas* comes only after *karma yoga, upasana yoga* and Vedantic inquiry. And unbroken love toward God is the bedrock conviction "I am limitless. I abide in the self as the self."

50. "Such a person certainly goes beyond *Maya* and helps the world to cross."

"Such a person" means someone who subjects his or her self to the complete devotional process outlined here. He or she avoids worldly company, engages in *satsang,* follows *karma yoga* in its entirety and takes up rigorous inquiry when the mind has become contemplative. Finally, after assimilating the knowledge of the *Vedas,* he is free to discard them. He can confidently claim:

> "I am not the mind, the intellect, thought or the ego. I am not the organ of hearing, tasting, smelling or seeing. I am not the sky, the earth, the fire or the air. I am the ever-pure blissful consciousness. I am Shiva, I am Shiva." (*Nivanasatkam,* verse 1)

If there is any doubt about it, Narada gives a guarantee. He says "certainly" you will cross. Having crossed, you can now help others to cross.

Chapter IV

The Definition of Non-Dual Love

ALTHOUGH NON-DUAL LOVE cannot be defined, it can be directly experienced by removing the obstacles to it, once self-ignorance is destroyed by the teachings. This chapter touts the value of self-inquiry and contrasts conditional and unconditional love.

51. "The essential nature of pure love of God is beyond description."

Because reality is non-dual existence/consciousness/love, devotion and love are non-different. However, since in worldly parlance the word "love" applies to objects and is mingled with desire for objects, we need to understand that in this context love is devotion toward the self. Yes, dualistic devotion is associated with desire, but this desire is the foremost qualification for *moksa* and the discovery of the non-dual love that is the nature of the self. Love is not a feeling, although it becomes a feeling when it flows through the human heart. But the feeling of love depends on the *guna* at play in the heart at any time, so it seems to change. The love that is the self is unchanging, limitless – "bliss." The best words to describe it are perfect satisfaction, perfect self-confidence and fullness.

It is love that is not dependent on an object. When I say I love an object, I am saying that in the presence of an object I feel happy, which implies that I am unhappy in the presence of certain other objects. The love that I am is always present and is constantly experienced internally. It expresses outwardly all the time in terms of the objects I pay attention to. It is manifested fullness.

No Cause-Effect Relationship

But *Maya* creates the following problem: when I experience a connection between the circumstances in which my internal love is manifested as a feeling of love, I implicitly posit a cause-effect relationship. Thereafter my aim becomes to have the loving feeling happen all the time, which creates a futile struggle. It is impossible to feel good always, because feelings take place in the time-bound aspect of reality (*mithya*) where nothing is the same from one moment to the next.

If I feel love in the presence of a person, I try to keep that person close to me all the time and a story forms. If I feel it in the presence of an animal, I want to keep it as a pet. If I feel it when I come to India, I become an India addict. The belief that love is associated with objects is called *śamsara* and is the cause of suffering.

Two Types of Bliss (*Ananda*)

The *Taittiriya Upanishad* points out that there are two types of bliss/love: original bliss of the self (*bimbananda*) and reflected bliss (*pratibimbananda*), or object-bliss.

Object-bliss (1) is experiential because it requires an object, (2) is temporary because objects come and go, and (3) comes in grades. It is called *priya* when I feel love at the thought of an object or in the presence of any object. *Priya* is subtle and does not produce strong emotions. It is called *moda* when I have obtained the object and can call it "mine." *Moda* produces a feeling of attachment. It is called *pramoda* when I connect with the object emotionally or physically and experience the intense pleasure of contact.

These states of experiential love do not apply to original *ananda*. The original love that I am is not a feeling as we think of feelings, but it is a feeling-like experience of pure satisfaction that is independent of objects. It is indefinable and indescribable, because we only have words for specific objects, not for non-objects, the self. What kind of word describes everything that is? When we say that original love is not experienceable, we mean that it is not experienceable as an object, not that it is not experienceable. It is experienced always, whether we "feel" it emotionally or not. When the mind is purified, it is felt as a constant positive presence.

Everyone knows or should know that object-love is not real love. In *Bhaja Govindam* Shankaracharya says (verse 4):

> "As long as a man is fit and able to support his family, see the affection those around him show. But his loved ones pay him no mind when his body totters due to old age."

Swami Paramarthananda says, "We say, 'honey, honey,' but when the money goes, the honey goes. At one time, I loved you and later I unlove you. Reflected love is temporary and it is graded." We may not admit it, but if we are asked to rank our love objects we can easily do so. I love my body first because without it I can't experience anything. I love my job second because it allows me to have a wife. I love my wife third because she gives me children and takes care of them. I love my children fourth, my house fifth, my dog sixth, my sister seventh, my car eighth, my friends ninth, my country tenth, etc.

Original limitless love (*prema*) is my nature. Shankaracharya analyzes it in his commentary on the final verse of the *Brihadaranyaka Upanishad* (3.9) in which he says, "This supreme original self (existence-consciousness-bliss) supports us in future births and in this birth also. It is the ultimate support of the self-realized liberated ones who are established in it by knowing it. It does not act, but every action, great and small, depends on it. It is the goal for which all people strive and the essential eternal self of all things and beings. Everything we value is due to it."

Even the love we have for our body is temporary. We love it as long as it serves our purposes. Under certain conditions, the body reflects bliss, but when it contacts an incurable disease we hope that it will die quickly.

I Can and I Can't Experience Love

Original pure love is (1) not a part, product or property of the body or mind. (2) It is an independent principle that pervades the body and mind when the conditions are ideal, making the body feel good and the mind a loving mind. (3) It is not limited by the boundaries of the body/mind/sense complex and (4) continues to exist even after the mind is resolved in deep sleep. We all love deep sleep because there is no suffering in it and we experience the bliss/love that is the nature of the self. (5) Pure love is experienced always, but it is inaccessible as an object, not because it is absent, but because there is no medium for it to express.

Only when the difference between pure love and reflected love is clear does the statement that it is indescribable make sense. The *Taittiriya Upanishad* (2.9.1) says, "The mind and speech return back from it baffled, as they are not able to grasp and describe it."

If you are asked to describe yourself, not your body or your story, you can only say, "I exist. I am conscious." If you can say "I am" you can say "I am love" because love is the nature of the "I."

I, love, cannot be experienced as an object, but when I experience objects I am experiencing myself reflected in them. Contrary to the silly teachings of many modern non-dualists, objects exist. If they did not exist, they could not be experienced. Objects, reflected existence, are always available for experience. When you say the wall is, the chair is, the table is and so forth, you are experiencing the self in the form of reflected existence; the is-ness of a table is a reflection of the self in the name and form of a table. So reflected is-ness is experienced as the world of objects. Similarly, reflected consciousness can be experienced in the physical body. Reflected happiness can also be experienced. Reflected happiness is experienced whenever I feel happy in the presence of an object, chocolate cake, for instance. The cake is sugar and other carbohydrates, but the bliss is me.

Liberation, which is self-knowledge, which is tantamount to non-dual love, is simply claiming my identity as love, based on the understanding of the difference between original love and its reflection.

When and Where Anyone Experiences Love, I Experience Love

I can say, "I exist and I am conscious," but can I say that I love everything? An ignorant person doesn't realize that when he loves an object, he is experiencing his own love nature and attributes the love to the object. An enlightened person knows that as he experiences objects – life is just a constant experience of objects – he is experiencing the existence, the consciousness, the happiness and the love of himself alone. He says, "I experience love everywhere in every object. When anyone experiences love, it is me experiencing love." As it says in the *Bhagavad Gita* (6.29), "He sees all beings in the self and the self in all beings. And how does he 'see'? He knows."

52. "Trying to describe the experience of pure love of God is like a mute trying to describe a particular taste."

Assuming you can speak, once you know the self all you can utter are superlatives: fantastic, wonderful, incredible!!! No matter how many exclamation points you put at the end your sentences, they are all woefully inadequate. But you can discover it in the form of the hard and fast knowledge "I am the self." It can only be claimed in this way because you are always experiencing it as the "I." Dualists who want to experience God struggle with this problem. Their prayers are full of longing and scolding. They lament, "Why don't you reveal yourself to me?" The one who is doing the longing is God under the spell of apparent ignorance.

53. "Occasionally, pure love of God is revealed in a qualified person."

This highest love, which is permanent, ungraded, non-experiential and my very nature, can only be discovered or claimed through an appropriate means. If discovering myself as pure existence requires a means, then discovering myself as pure love also requires a means. It cannot be discovered by sitting with closed eyes and singing devotional hymns. Chanting the names of God may help me discover reflected love, but when the chanting ends and I go back to my humdrum life, the bliss/love ends. Singing the praises of God is desirable because it creates a *sattvic* mind in which the qualifications for teaching flower, but it will not set you free. If you experience love coming from *Isvara,* it is still reflected love because it will end too. The God-object can be a source of bliss, but not lasting bliss. You have to discover that what you worship "there" is what you are "here."

Isvara's Law of Love

So how can you come to know it? Inquire into what you love most. Here is an inquiry from the *Brihadaranyaka Upanishad* (1.4.8):

> "This self is dearer than a son, dearer than wealth, dearer than everything else and is one's innermost being. Should a person holding the self as the dearest say to someone who says anything else is dearest, he is competent to truthfully say, 'What you hold dear will die one day. Meditate on the self alone as the dearest, not on mortal loved ones.'"

Dualistic devotees are not interested in Vedanta, preferring instead to worship and sing the praises of an objective God as they conceive of it. But you cannot get what you already have by action, because no action is eternal. Narada himself practiced dualistic devotion for years but it did not give him eternal love, so he went to a *guru* and learned the difference between reflected love and the love that he is (*satya/mithya*).

Chandogya Upanishad, 7.24.1:

> "The limitless self is That in which one sees nothing else, hears nothing else and understands nothing else. The finite world is that in which one sees otherness, hears otherness and understands otherness. That which is infinite is immortal, and that which is finite is mortal. Oh, revered one, wherein does the self rest? In its own majesty – or not in majesty."

Self-inquiry, by way of investigation of the great *Upanishadic mantras,* is the path to discover the simple fact that "I am pure love."

Samsaris, people who look for love from people who are looking for love, obviously don't know what love is. If you find yourself in this situation, please consider Vedanta's first teaching: love is not in objects. As long as others look upon you as a source of joy, love will flow from them. The moment you stop being a source of joy – or worse, when you become a burden to them – their love will disappear like a gradually depleting bank account. You can't blame them; it is the nature of *samsara* and they think *samsara* is real. Husbands and wives always pray that each other will be healthy because sickness puts a burden on love and causes it slowly to erode. It is *Isvara's* law that love only flows toward a source of joy. You will only be loved as long as you are interesting and useful. Additionally, your love for an object will only last as long as the object conforms to your likes and dislikes, which are not under your control unless you are a *karma yogi,* in which case you can successfully love another living being. But what is the point if I am the love that I seek in others? So on any account, depending on an object for love is futile.

Once I discover my self as love, I have tapped into an endless source. In discovering love for and from myself, in discovering that everyone is essentially my self, my love becomes permanent and universal. Only self-knowledge allows me to discover permanent love. Once I know who I am, I am not concerned if I am loved by others or whether "my" love of them is reciprocated. But I helplessly love everyone because I have no choice about it. Pure love is *Isvara* loving through me as me. It expresses as my very presence. People are attracted to me because the love in me awakens the love in them. I need not consciously behave in a loving way to convince myself or others that I know who I am, like so many self-proclaimed enlightened people. My *jiva* can just be what it is, and the love lifts them up.

Many claim to know the self, either as an object or as the subject, but this does not necessarily mean that their hearts are pure enough to express it purely. In fact most modern "enlightened" people who have stumbled on the self via experiential means have not done serious work on their *jivas.* Or if they have and they tout enlightenment as an experience, they actually aren't free, because enlightenment is freedom from the doer, the one inclined to claim enlightenment. It is dangerous to trust such people with your devotion, because they are not qualified to receive it, meaning that it will be retained by their egos and used according to their desires, not passed on to *Isvara.* This is why Narada points out that "there is danger of a fall." *Vasanas,* positive and negative, are extremely conservative and are not immediately transformed with the dawn of self-knowledge. So if a person's heart/mind was not properly purified when the knowledge "I am the self" happened, beware. To increase your dependence on them, "enlightened" people often have clever ways of allaying the inbuilt fear that comes when you surrender to another person. Add the innate gullibility of a wanting person and you have a recipe for disaster. The most common myth perpetuated by so-called enlightened people is the idea that there are no qualifications for enlightenment. If there are no qualifications for enlightenment, there are no qualifications for enlightened people. But to protect seekers from unqualified teachers, Vedanta says that if you want to want to experience and know pure love, you will find it in qualified souls.

A Qualified Enlightened Person

You need to be qualified for *moksa*. Even if you realize who you are but are denied the fruit – perfect non-egoic satisfaction and satisfaction with a seemingly endlessly dissatisfied ego – then you have not finished your spiritual work and you have to requalify. A qualified person is discriminating, dispassionate, disciplined and endowed with a burning desire for liberation. This means that his or her mind is pure. A pure mind is one in which the *vasanas* have been neutralized by spiritual work, both *karma yoga* and *jnana yoga*. When the mind is pure, the love that is one's nature expresses in a pure, non-attached, discriminating way. So our standard is very high. This is why the *sampradaya,* the tradition, has continued in its original clarity and purity for thousands of years. The cooked-up modern "lineages," which are not lineages at all but are simply attempts to lend gravitas to ad hoc "teachers" and "teachings," will not rate even a minor footnote in the fullness of time, because they are contaminated by the unpurified personalities of the *gurus.* Love is impersonal and pure because the self is not a person. Even the "greats" in our tradition, Shankaracharya, for instance, only claimed that they were one small link in the tradition. Their teachings were never theirs; they only emphasized or elucidated certain aspects of the eternal *Upanishadic mantras* that are the foundation for the teachings. Pure unconditional love shines only when self-knowledge is complete and firm. As it says in the *Bhagavad Gita* (7.3): "Among thousands of human beings, a rare one strives for liberation. Even among those who strive, a rare one knows me in reality."

54. "Pure love of God is devoid of material qualities and desires, manifests more and more every moment, is uninterrupted and is always experienced as one's innermost consciousness."

If your heart is not pure, your love will be contaminated by materialistic qualities and desires. Witness the tragicomic parade of apparently inspired but corrupt *swamis* and *lamas* that burst upon the Western spiritual scene since the sixties, that were feted and lauded by thousands of gullible seekers yet ended up disgraced. Where are their "teachings" and their lineages now? Is it any wonder that the general public is totally cynical about spirituality? With rare exceptions, even the purity of their apparently more benign recent variants – the Neo-Advaita non-dualists – is also suspect. A case could be made that even the modern "love" *gurus* are not necessarily popular because of the purity of their love but because they display and validate emotional neediness, which they define as love. You need only look as far as their resistance to letting their followers move on to other teachers to understand that their love is contaminated by fear of loss and desire for recognition.

This infinite and unconditional love, which in a qualified *mahatma* is directed toward everyone, is free of qualities. It is not contaminated by desire (*rajas*) or fear (*tamas*). It is not even pure, insofar as pure implies impure. It is not *sattvic, rajasic* or *tamasic,* because it is discovered through the self, which is free of the *gunas*. As Krishna says (*Gita,* 14.19-20):

> "When one understands the doer to be none other than the *gunas* and knows the self, which is beyond the *gunas,* one attains my nature. Having gone beyond the three *gunas,* which are the cause of rebirth, a person becomes free from birth, death, old age and sorrow, and attains immortality."

This non-dual devotion, this infinite and unconditional love, is non-demanding and devoid of materialistic desire. Demanding love is conditional love, not essential and real love. If I love you because you have a pretty face, I don't love you for the beauty that makes beauty beautiful. I do not see you. If I stop loving you when you no longer do what I want, my love is not real.

People who know who they are don't want anything from anyone. Suffering people stop worshiping the Lord when their suffering is not ameliorated by their prayers. Materialistic people cease to pray if their prayers don't bear fruit. Even knowledge-seekers get disappointed if they don't get enlightened when they think they should. But enlightened people don't even want things that *Isvara* tries to give them, because they are satisfied in themselves. They always "want" only what they have, which means self-love is desireless.

Why do I love *Isvara* if I am not getting anything in return? Because *Isvara* is love and love is its own reward; it is good in any situation because *Isvara* and I happen to be one and the same. For me, self-love includes *Isvara*. Self-love includes everything because the self is non-dual. Therefore natural self-love becomes *Isvara*-love and it becomes universal love because *Isvara* and the universe are included in the one, all-pervading self that I am.

This love is subtler than the subtlest, beyond all objects, is always present and always experienced as "I am."

All these *sutras* can only be properly understood if we remember the fundamental Vedantic equation: existence is equal to awareness, awareness is equal to bliss and bliss is equal to love. These words are synonyms. They do not refer to four "parts" of the self; they are the self manifesting differently in different media.

In the material world, for example, the existence "aspect" alone is manifest. If you say the wall is, you should know that its "is-ness" belongs to the self. But a wall cannot manifest love, because it has no reflecting medium, a Subtle Body. We experience both existence and awareness in the physical body because the physical body – except the hair and nails – is pervaded by the Subtle Body. When conditions are conducive – for instance, your loved ones are acting exactly as you would like them to, the mind manifests existence, awareness and love toward whomever is responsible for making the mind conducive. This is not the bliss of the Subtle Body, the mind, but the bliss of the self reflected in the mind. Existence, awareness, bliss and love all belong to me, the self, expressing differently at different times and under different conditions. You cannot separate who you are from what you know, because reality is non-dual. This love, then, is in the form of direct and ever-experienced self-knowledge. You cannot will yourself to love unconditionally; you can only discover who you are and you will see that your love is, has been and always will be unconditional.

If non-dual love is unchanging and continuous as scripture says, why does the verse say that it increases at every moment? As self-knowledge develops into the unshakable conviction "I am the limitless self" owing to increasing insight into the true nature of reality and subjectivity is reduced by objective analysis, my love for myself and others grows and grows. Actually, it seemingly grows, meaning that the *jiva* experiences it more and more intensely as obstructing *vasanas* in the form of the ill-considered misconceptions, beliefs, opinions, expectations and delusions that condition the reflecting media – the Subtle Body – recede.

The light of a full moon in a cloudless daylight sky, in the early evening and at midnight is constant, but is unseen in daylight, appears as a pale orb in the early evening and shines brightly in the dead of night. We don't see the love in others or in ourselves when we are caught up in *samsara*. As *rajas* and *tamas* recede owing to the practice of *karma yoga* and *jnana yoga,* we start to feel the pale light of love toward ourselves and others. When the mind becomes highly *sattvic* owing to firm self-knowledge, our love intensifies and magnifies, and it is abundantly clear that each of us is an embodiment of pure non-dual love.

Love Is Discovered, Never Produced

Even the most heinous murderer is capable of lavishing the tenderest love on his wife and children because pure love is the nature of every sentient being. If you want to be loved and you cannot understand why you aren't loved, it is because the love that you are is obstructed by some impurity - anger, desire, selfishness, pride, etc. You cannot ask someone to love you, but you will be loved by all if your likes and dislikes have been neutralized by self-knowledge. Spiritual life is uncovering, never creating. Even if you have a powerful experience of non-dual love, it will fade unless you are committed to purifying your mind.

55. "Having discovered non-dual love, you see only the self everywhere, hear the self in every word, speak only of the self and think only of the self."

As long as you think that non-dual love is a particular substance or energy only available in the form of a unique experience, you will imagine that the actual physical, emotional and intellectual way you experience life will be fundamentally altered when you discover who you are.

Does the verse mean that if you saw a tree before you discovered who you are you won't see the tree afterwards; instead, you will see "the self"? If so, you may wonder, "What exactly does the self look like?" Does it mean that when someone speaks you won't hear the words themselves, you will hear only the self? If so, is Narada saying that the self has a unique sound - the sound of the infinite (*nada brahman*) - experienced only by the enlightened? If you have a mind prone to magical thinking, you might imagine that self-realized people live in a special state, a unique spiritual "world" far removed from this one, a "transcendental sky," for instance. If so, how will I tie my shoes and park my car when I don't see shoes and cars? Will the Internal Revenue Service take "the self" as payment for my taxes, since that is all I have?

Love is not an object like an emotion. Common sense tells us that the mind is given to all types of emotions. If everything is non-dual love, it cannot be a particular feeling, because no feeling is present in all beings all the time. Even self-realized people express varieties of emotions. It can't be a thought for the same reason. We can only understand this verse if we understand that non-dual love is the nature of the self; it is my existence/consciousness/wholeness/bliss. It is original, causeless and abiding happiness.

> "Those whose minds are disciplined through inquiry perceive the self in all beings and all beings in the self, and value everything equally. I [the self] am not lost to those who see me everywhere and see everything in me. I am always aware of them and they of me." (*Bhagavad Gita*, 6.29-30)

In this context, seeing and perceiving are not experiential terms. How do the enlightened "see"? How do they "perceive"? They know. When they see an object, feeling or thought, they know that it is not a stand-alone object with its own particular essence. They see it as the self appearing as an object, feeling or thought. They know that the feeling or thought is not real, that it does not define or validate the self, and hence they remain free of the experiences generated by objects.

With reference to material things, I am available as the very existence of those things. With reference to sentient beings, I am available as the very consciousness of those beings. And when I see the existence in an object, love is also there because existence and love are non-different. If I don't see love in someone, I know that even though the person is me – love – the conditions required for that love to reflect and be experienced are not present, because the mind is dull (*tamasic*) or agitated (*rajasic*).

Even if a person hates me, I know that although the love that he is is present, it is not manifest, because it has been hijacked by his likes and dislikes. Ironically, if I give him what he wants, the love that he is will flow to me. And I know that he withholds his love because it pleases him to do so, which only goes to show that his love for himself is non-dual because it transcends his dislike of me.

An enlightened person knows that everyone has love in the form of the self at all times – unobstructed or obstructed, manifest or unmanifest – because just as there is only consciousness and just as there is only existence, there is only love. So if I am enlightened, everything I hear or think is the self. When the verse says that enlightened people think of the self all the time, it does not mean that they have only one thought: "I am existence/awareness." If they are thinking of the self all the time in this way, how can they perform worldly transactions, since each transaction requires a unique thought? It means that even as they transact with objects they are aware of the "love light" that illumines every transaction and they know "I am that ever-full, ever-present light."

The *Bhagavad Gita* (3.17) says, "Nothing needs to be done for the person who loves the self alone, is happy and contented with the self alone." This verse does not mean that enlightened people sit unmoving in silence but that they are full of love, so there is no need for them to do anything to get the love of others to prove to themselves that they are lovable. Every action is soaked in non-demanding love.

56. "Secondary devotional service is of three kinds, according to which of the *gunas* predominates at any time or according to the motivation – distress, desire or knowledge – that brings one to devotion."

Verses 51 to 55 speak of non-dual love, point out that love and devotion and the self are non-different, and that it is discovered through self-knowledge. Verse 56 returns to the topic of conditional love, secondary devotion as a means to non-dual love.

If you don't know where you are going, how will you know when you have arrived? The modern spiritual world is terribly confusing because the nature of the goal, non-dual love and the means to attain it – self inquiry – is never clarified by the teachers. Even after exposure to many non-dual *satsangs* and non-dual teachers, seekers are rudderless, unable to proceed for want of clear knowledge. No matter how many times I am told that I am awareness and not the body-mind, without a proven means of self-knowledge I am incapable of unconditionally loving myself and others. What is the point, since the innermost need of everyone is the need to love and be loved?

You can argue that secondary devotion is at least as important as primary non-dual devotion, insofar as without it you won't discover who you really are.

We have already pointed out that without dualistic devotion in the form of *karma yoga* and *upasana yoga* (meditation on *Isvara*) you will not appreciate the scripture's statement that you are love and only love. This verse discusses secondary devotion from the point of view of the *gunas* and the underlying motivations as it is presented in the *Bhagavad Gita*.

How devotion expresses depends on the nature of the three subconscious tendencies (*vasanas*) that control our behavior: *sattva, rajas* and *tamas*.[21] The field of existence is comprised of three energies which are continually evolving and involving, weaving in and out of our consciousness like strands of fiber in a rope binding us to the world. Each Subtle Body is comprised of all three, but tends to be anchored in one or the other. Devotional practice is meant to purify *rajas* and *tamas,* thereby increasing the relative proportion of *sattva,* the power that makes knowledge – including God-knowledge – possible.

Tamas is a veiling energy, the power of inertia, darkness and sleep, manifesting materially as matter, physical substance. Psychologically, it is the sleepy dullness we feel after a big meal, hearty exercise or a day at the office. The unflattering terms "sloth," "laziness" and "stupidity" describe this common state of mind.

Perception takes place when a perceived object and the mind of the perceiving subject are bathed in light. For example, to see a tree, physical light is essential. To register the perception, psychic light – reflected consciousness – is necessary. If the mind is dull or sleepy, knowledge will be inaccurate. When the mind is under the spell of this dark energy, our critical faculties are suspended and we're unaware of what's going on and incapable of assimilating knowledge.

Tamas – the Veiling Power

The *tamasic* mind, rooted firmly in duality, is incapable of non-dual knowledge. At best, with the help of *rajas,* the projecting power, it personifies God as an all-powerful being with humanlike characteristics, a "jealous" God, for instance, that needs to be worshiped fearfully and slavishly as a child worships its parents, the "Father" in heaven. Such a mind is naturally fearful, superstitious and prone to magical thinking. It readily believes in ghosts, evil spirits, poltergeists, sin and the Devil.

The dark energy dictates a commitment to formulas, especially ritual, and literal interpretation of scripture. Ignorance loves organization, swelling the ranks of churches worldwide. Because thinking for oneself is considered willful and disobedient, the *tamasic* devotee is easily manipulated by false

[21]A comprehensive discussion of the the "*gunas,*" the qualities that color psyche and matter and their relationship to purification of mind, is found in *The Essence of Enlightenment.*

prophets and power-hungry priests, and is attracted to cults of personality. To question or attack his or her narrow-minded faith is to gain an enemy for life. Religious history is replete with examples of the excesses wreaked from this state of mind. On the upside, *tamasic* faith is unshakable, capable of withstanding life's pinpricks and her major crises. The conviction that God exists is steady, deep and heartfelt.

Rajas – the Projecting Power

Rajas, the mode of passion, is a projecting, striving, grasping, aggressive energy. Under its influence the mind is continually roiled with distracting thoughts and emotions which conceal the self and cut off the flow of love from within. The extroverted *rajasic* mind, rarely self-aware, views the world as the source of all meaning and searches passionately for objects, people and situations that will supposedly fulfill it.

The mind under *rajas'* power makes the devotee vain, self-centered and not above asking God for worldly things – money, sex, power, position, etc. The perennial theory of abundance and prosperity is tailor-made for passionate devotees who tend to be status- and image-conscious, and view devotion as evidence of spiritual attainment, often using it to impress or humiliate others. Scratch the surface of this type and you have someone more interested in presenting a devotional front to the world than a devotional heart to God. Unlike the steady dependability of the *tamasic* type, the active devotee will change faiths, teachings, teachers and practices at the drop of a hat.

However, once he or she is committed to *karma yoga* and self-inquiry, the *rajasic* devotee becomes a dynamic bundle of energy, capable of rapid progress. His or her businesslike concern with results and passionate love of *Isvara* attracts *Isvara* like nothing else. The ambitious belief that self-realization is possible allows the devotee to transform *rajas* into *sattva,* the highest of the three secondary types of devotion and gateway to non-dual love. Both *rajas* and *tamas* are material, not spiritual, energies because they direct the mind to the world rather than God.

Sattva – the Revealing Power

The third strand of universal energy is *sattva,* which perfectly reflects consciousness. Knowledge is impossible without consciousness, and the mind in which this power predominates easily gains clear understanding and pure love of truth. The quintessential spiritual power, *sattva,* confers intelligence, peace, curiosity, beauty, knowledge and awareness. *Sattvic* individuals are the world's creative motor, providing society with inspiration, ideas and ideals.

The "light" element is the foundation for a high and noble non-dual devotion because it allows the heart to know and experience God's subtle radiance.

The devotee situated in the mode of light enjoys the ego of a superior soul, one who knows more and loves unconditionally, one attached to purity and goodness, the golden chain tethering him or her to life. However, *sattva* is devotionally desirable because the veil separating the devotee and God is so thin.

If your mind is predominantly *sattvic,* it will orient itself toward spiritual growth through self-knowledge. You will work on the qualifications, try to find a qualified teacher and give up your interest in pursuing spiritual experiences. It makes *Isvara's* job easy because *Isvara* need only remove your ignorance and change your mind. *Rajasic* devotion is egoic and possessive, as it is centered around gaining worldly objects: relationships, family, recognition, power, career, financial and other benefits. It puts a lot of stress on *Isvara* because it requires *Isvara* to manipulate the *dharma* field so that external circumstances align with your likes and dislikes. It is fraught with frustration. *Rajas* even bedevils inquirers who are uninterested in worldly benefits, causing them to chase spiritual experiences. While *rajasic* devotion inclines the devotee in a positive direction, *tamasic* devotion is negative and blind. *Tamasic* individuals want happiness, but when the object of their desires is blocked they set out to destroy the obstacle because they can't wait for *Isvara* to remove the block. The world is presently witnessing a fine example of *tamasic* devotion in the form of ISIS, the movement to establish the Caliphate. There is no doubt that these individuals are devoted to God as they see it; most *jihadis* have calluses on their foreheads from repeatedly touching the earth during their prayers. Rabidly dualistic, you will get no peace and love from them, as they are firmly entrenched in an "us versus them" mentality: "If you are not with us, you are against us, and if you are against us, you obviously don't love God, and anyone who doesn't love God needs to be controlled or destroyed because the purpose of life is to establish the kingdom of God here on earth."

The fourth type of devotee – the non-dual – established in Chapter VII, verse 16 of the *Gita,* is not discussed here, because the verse is unfolding secondary devotion (*guna bhakti*). Generally, devotion is explained with reference to types of individuals (the suffering, the craving and inquiring) but it is not helpful to stereotype yourself or others. It is best to think of them as devotional tendencies within your own mind that need to be transformed by *karma yoga* and inquiry: destructive *tamasic* impulses should be sublimated into *rajasic* desires for purification, and *sattvic* tendencies converted into a burning desire for self-knowledge, not merely a desire for pleasure and convenience. However, since the text presents the stages of devotion as psychological types, we will explain these tendencies in this manner.

57. "Each succeeding type of devotee is superior to the preceding type."

1. The Opportunist

The lowest type of devotee is fear-oriented (*tamas*) and opportunistic (*rajas*), only worshiping God when he is distressed and in trouble. Because he lacks *sattva,* his mind is dull and he is uninterested in liberation or self-inquiry.

2. The Businessman

Although he is also opportunistic, he is a cut above the miserable opportunist because his emotional state is more positive and his understanding of God is slightly more refined. Although he is actually a *samsari,* we will dignify him with the term "devotee" because he realizes that success in any field depends on factors not directly under his control and appeals to God, who controls the field, for help. He might reasonably be called a business devotee who makes self-serving deals with God: "I will make a donation to the church if you give me what I want. I will fast once a week if you see to it that my daughter gets into a good university." He is also not interested in liberation or self-inquiry.

A slightly more evolved variant of the businessman is the do-gooding, helping type with a psychological orientation: life coaches, psychologists – particularly transpersonal psychologists – and "healers." Because they have more *sattva,* they may be interested in self-inquiry, not because they want *moksa,* although they often pay lip service to it, but because they appreciate Vedanta's wealth of psychological knowledge and its techniques for transforming the mind. For Vedanta to set you free, you need to expose your mind to the complete teaching. If you pick and choose only the teachings that fit into your system, you will not grow spiritually.

It is common for people to misuse Vedanta. Indeed in India there are even devotees who study Vedanta for business management reasons. *Karma yoga* and *triguna vibhava yoga* have definite business applications.

3. The Intellectual

This is a pure-minded, intellectually curious seeker of knowledge who has a spiritual *vasana* but does not have a burning desire for liberation. He or she thinks liberation is a wonderful idea but entertains only an academic interest in Vedanta. These devotees can often be found in the philosophy or religious studies departments of universities and may write their theses on particularly obscure and advanced texts, the *Brahma Sutras,* for instance. Usually, this kind of devotee has a comfortable *dharmic* life and fears compromising it because scripture encourages renunciation of action and the fruits of action. He does not want to rock the boat and believes he will go for *moksa* when he retires. He is unlikely to do so, because when retirement rolls around, one's worldly tendencies are so deeply entrenched there is little enthusiasm for confronting and transforming them.

4. The Experiencer

Above the intellectual is the anti-intellectual devotee who badly wants liberation but feels that there are many ways to attain it: "All roads lead to Rome." They don't; only self-knowledge is liberation because the devotee is already free. This devotee may practice Patanjali *yoga* with the aim of getting in a special *samadhi, kundalini yoga* for mystic experiences, Transcendental Meditation, Neo-Advaita or one of the devotional paths, Krishna Consciousness, for instance. He or she may actually follow a Vedantic *guru* like Ramana Maharshi or Nisargadatta, yet ignore the teacher's statements that indicate that the self can only be gained by knowledge, and persistently chase the "final" epiphany! Because he thinks *moksa* is a happening or a destination, he tries to produce it by pilgrimages, chanting, austerities, meditation, reading and other rituals. Neo-Advaita *satsangs* appeal to this type of devotee because they are all about experiencing the self, not self-knowledge. It is a frustrating path. He does not value self-knowledge, and therefore is averse to Vedanta. However, if his desire persists, he will eventually stumble on Vedanta by default.

5. The Inquirer

The highest type of devotee is one who has a burning desire for liberation and a deep commitment to self-inquiry. He is like a gravely ill person seeking a cure for a pernicious disease. He takes a professional attitude toward inquiry, is obsessed with scripture and follows the suggestions of the teacher with great diligence. Usually this person cannot live in society and decides to drop out because he understands that the path of inquiry requires one-pointed concentration.

As it says in the *Mundaka Upanishad* (1.2.12):

> "When, after examining the entirety of one's life experiences, one realizes that everlasting happiness cannot be gained through the pursuit of objects and the results of actions, he is advised to humbly approach a proper teacher who is learned in the *Vedas,* and making that knowledge his own, revel in it."

The greatest devotee is a desperate self-inquirer. His situation is like a person whose hair is on fire. If there is water nearby, whether it is a freezing mountain stream or a hot polluted swamp, he will jump right in without first checking the temperature or the sanitary conditions. Worldly situations are of no interest to him. The Buddha, for example, was a rich prince who walked away from the high life without a second thought and subjected himself to untold hardship in his quest for freedom. These are fortunate people. If they have good *karma* they will end up keeping the company of a *mahatma* and take to inquiry (*vichara*); if not, after much hard work on many different paths they will usually return to the world to marry and start a career.

58. "Success is easier to attain by informal devotion than by any other means."
Compared to all other paths and practices, it is easiest to begin one's quest with devotion, an idea that appears in the *Gita* (9.30-31) where the self speaks these words:

> "Even a person who violates *dharma* and who worships the self should be looked on as a saint, for he is clear that the purpose of life is liberation. In time, through his worship, he will become a noble soul and will certainly attain lasting peace. My devotee never perishes."

This verse does not mean that informal devotion is the easiest way to freedom, which is the view of the devotional schools, only that it is a good starting point. It is not a good place to end. Informal devotion is the easiest because one needn't know how to perform any of the rituals necessary for formal dualistic devotion, which requires some knowledge of the *Vedas*. So it is easier than *karma yoga,* meditation and Vedanta.

It is easiest because the only capital investment required is love and love is the nature of the self, so everyone is well endowed. Even before we love God, self-love is present, although it is only directed to the objects, people and things connected to us. Even misers love money, the weak love power and the ignorant love knowledge. Even animals have self-love, as evidenced by the fact that they run away when threatened. So love need not be acquired, only directed toward God. Love of objects is emotional love. When emotion is directed to God, usually a personal deity, it is transformed into devotion, which gradually ameliorates painful experiences and produces peace of mind. When the mind becomes peaceful, inquiry comes to the surface and blesses the devotee. But to start, you do not even need to know how to think to practice it; it is available to the illiterate and the educated alike. In whatever way the devotee chooses to worship the self, the self will respond by strengthening his or her faith. Although simple devotion needs to eventually be converted to faith pending the result of inquiry into the self, blind faith is better than doubt and distrust, which destroys spiritual growth before it even sprouts.

59. "Devotion is easiest because it does not depend on any other authority; it is self-validating."

Vedanta encourages dualistic devotion as a stepping stone to non-dual devotion, but also points out that dualists neglect inquiry and therefore miss out on the ultimate form of devotion. If a devotee wants to be free of the sense of separation from God, he needs to depend on the authority of the scripture, since God created scripture solely to erase the devotee's sense of duality. Having said that, all you need to start worshiping is to start worshiping.

60. "Furthermore, devotion is the embodiment of peace and supreme joy."

You feel happy when you worship your self in any form. Your self-esteem grows no end because the self, your best friend, blesses you with its love. Dualists understand this fact. "Jesus [a symbol for the self] loves you" means that when you invoke God with your prayers, God, your very essence, loves you back, which is experienced as peace, joy and contentment.

Love of objects is conditional, but love of God, even if it is initially devotion to God in a particular form, is unconditional, from both *Isvara's* and the devotee's perspective. *Isvara* doesn't care if you are a good person or a bad person, because *Isvara* sees you as non-separate. So don't think that you are unworthy in the sight of God. And when you feel the joy of worship, you become unconditionally committed because the pursuit of happiness is every person's sole motivation. Devotees are smart because they don't misplace their love. If you love an object, at some point you will be disappointed, but if you love your self you will never be disappointed. There is nothing complicated about this kind of love; even the simple thought of God in the form of some symbol – a cuddly animal, for instance – invokes love, which brings peace, which in turn leads to inquiry.

61. "Once all worldly and spiritual duties are consigned to God, the devotee need not worry about gain and loss."

When you love someone, you become extremely curious about who they are. When you love God, you become extremely curious about your self. You may not be directly led to Vedanta, but your devotion to a particular form of the Lord will lead to an appreciation of life itself as the glory of the Lord.

When you see that God is everything, which is the essence of Vedanta, your sense of "I" and "mine" disappears. "I" and "mine" is the basis of the fear of loss, which is the greatest human sorrow, particularly the loss of loved ones. Your sense of duality disappears because Vedanta reveals the true nature of the "I." The "I" is ever-full love. If the devotee is *Isvara* and *Isvara* is the devotee, then every blessed thing belongs to me, which means that I am unaffected by anything and attached to nothing.

Devotional culture favors the use of the word "*Bhagavan*" in place of *Isvara,* the Vedantic term. *Bhaga* means "opulent wealth" and *van* means "the one who possesses." So *Bhagavan* is (1) all-powerful; nothing happens anywhere without the blessing of consciousness. It is (2) totally courageous, meaning it is capable of overcoming every obstacle that *Maya* creates. It is (3) totally famous; God's name endures from the beginning of creation to the end, whereas even the fame of "great" *jivas* is time-constrained. Furthermore, whatever fame or infamy a *jiva* enjoys is due to the reflected power and intelligence of the self. *Bhagavan* is (4) opulently wealthy; all objects are generated by *Maya* out of *Bhagavan's* "body," i.e. the substance of everything is consciousness, which means that every object that I apparently own actually belongs to the self. *Bhagavan* is (5) all-knowing, meaning that it is impossible to know anything unless consciousness is present, which it is always. And finally, *Bhagavan* is (6) totally dispassionate; it is completely free of the whole creation, which means that it is unaffected by whatever happens.

What Use Is God-Knowledge?

The more I appreciate my identity with *Bhagavan* the less possessive and vain I become. When I appreciate my non-separation from *Bhagavan* the more non-attached to what happens I become; my worries dry up. I also become more generous and compassionate because I know that nothing belongs to me and anyone in need is actually me. Freed of worry about results of my actions, property and love, I become a contributor, not an extractor, and stop begging and bribing God for things. I respond appropriately according to my nature and let things happen according to the law of *karma,* which is non-separate from *Bhagavan.* If at all I pray, I say, "Whatever has been decided by You will come to me according to my past actions. My only prayer is that moment to moment I will always offer unflinching devotion at your lotus feet." (*Mukundu Mala Stotra,* verse 5) If at all I pray, I pray for strength to face the inevitable losses that are part and parcel of life, and I gladly accept the courage that *Bhagavan* bestows in response to my prayer.

Knowing *Bhagavan,* you worship without desire and you can appreciate (and pity) how dualists with an incomplete knowledge of *Bhagavan,* full of desire for "heavenly" results, delude themselves into thinking that their sacred and secular rituals will produce lasting happiness. Devotion with knowledge endows the devotee with the strength to resist the worldly temptations (*vasanas*) that prevent inquiry.

62. "To attain non-dual devotion, do not abandon responsibilities in this world, but surrender the results of all actions to the Lord."

If you want the freedom that non-dual devotion confers, you cannot walk away from your life and become inactive. You need to stay where you are and do what you do in the *karma yoga* spirit, as it prepares the mind for inquiry. *Karma yoga* means that God gets to worry about the results of your actions, since results are God's business, not yours.

If you are a proper devotee, your service to the world is service to *Bhagavan.* You don't expect anything in return, but *Bhagavan* always rewards you. In fact devotional service is its own reward. Devotional service is service to whomever your *karma* brings into your energy field, and it highlights the ego's insatiable need for validation – read: gratitude. If your self-esteem is related to others' views of you, you have a lot of work to do. You should supply the gratitude you expect from others in the form of the gratitude to *Bhagavan* for the opportunity to serve. Yes, appreciation from others is always appreciated, but never seek it. It betrays a low sense of self-esteem. Furthermore, it is good manners to offer gratitude when someone gives you something unsolicited, and it is kind – noblesse oblige – to show gratitude when it is expected, but you are not doing others a favor by validating their need for validation, as you only validate their lack of self-appreciation.

Service is not a desire-oriented psychology. If you want to serve, you probably have a self-esteem issue: you want to think of yourself as a kind and generous, egoless person, which only means that you are not a kind and generous person. In the world do-gooders get a lot of respect, so you often see them causing all kinds of trouble with their unsolicited and well-intentioned meddling. Nobody should want to serve. You serve by responding to situations appropriately - or not. Situations are *Isvara,* the field of existence, asking for your participation. *Isvara* is not interested in gratitude. Gratitude is appropriate to *Jiva,* who is forever in *Isvara's* debt. Both the husband who expects gratitude for bringing home the bacon and the wife who expects gratitude for cooking it for the husband are not *karma yogis.* They are both simply doing *Isvara's* bidding.

63, 64. "Don't chase money or entertain yourself with sex. Don't compromise your values and don't quarrel with others. Relinquish false pride, hypocrisy and other vices."

One of the most important qualifications for inquiry is sense-control because the sense organs are the gateways to the world, which is always trying to gatecrash the mind. Once you let the world in, the mind is disturbed and incapable of discrimination. The mind needs to be inoculated from worldly viruses, the most dramatic of which are sex and money. So a devotee needs to be able to withdraw the sense organs from the objects "as a tortoise withdraws its limbs" when it is in danger. If not, self-knowledge will not stick. If you are unable to withdraw your senses from the objects, you face a big problem.

However, the verse does not say that you should be celibate or only have intercourse to procreate. It says that sex should not be thought of as entertainment. Sex is a beautiful way to express deep love for another person, but sex as entertainment is a sign of boredom. It means that you are not an entertaining person. Life itself should be interesting and exciting because you are on the greatest journey humanly possible. If it isn't and you restlessly crave excitement, you are a dull person, lacking imagination.

> "If you dwell on sense objects, a fancy toward them arises. From fantasy desire is born. If you want objects, anger is inevitable. Anger creates delusion, and you can't remember your purpose in life. If you can't remember why you are here,

you lose your discrimination, without which your soul dies."
(*Gita*, 2.62-63)

A devotee needs to filter what he sees and hears. If you don't, the world will produce thoughts unconducive to inquiry: lust, anger, greed and delusion. Since the media reflects the values of the society, and the society is exclusively interested in wealth and pleasure, the media should not be viewed as a friend. Sex sells and fear is the coin of the media realm. This injunction does not imply celibacy or penury, only careful monitoring of one's attention. A proverb says, "It is rare for a poor man to appreciate the value of wisdom. It is even more rare for a wise man to appreciate the value of wealth." We need money to live, but too much attention to it is spiritually counterproductive.

The Value of Values

The verse, which I have altered, actually says that one should avoid "atheists," which Vedanta defines as people who are uninterested in freedom and/or those who are willing to compromise their values for some worldly goal: sex, money, power, fame, etc. Finally, we should not think about people who don't like us, because such thoughts generate anger.

At the same time, we need to remain alert to the values that compromise inquiry and cultivate the values conducive to it. The following values are listed in the sixteenth chapter of the *Bhagavad Gita*.

1. Pride, Vanity, Conceit, Self-Glorification

A simple, factual self-respectfulness is a good quality. However, most of us have doubts about our adequacy. We secretly fear that we are not good enough and are unable to provide ourselves with the confidence we need to be happy with our lives. So we look to others to validate us. In order to gain validation, we are often tempted to exaggerate our qualifications and accomplishments so that others will think we are special and glorify us. If I am completely certain about my talents and abilities, I take them for granted and have no need for validation or support.

Demanding respect from others invites many disturbances because the one who asks for respect is not in control of the result. People give it for reasons known only to them. When their minds change, the validation is withdrawn and hurt arises. Any form of hurt is due to pride, an inflated ego, one that is excessively attached to what it thinks it knows, believes, possesses or how it looks. For example, body-conscious individuals who spend an inordinate amount of time grooming or calling attention to their bodies with expensive clothing, outlandish hairdos, tattoos and piercings often do so to attract attention they are incapable of giving themselves. Such egos, inflated by pride and vanity, invariably end up deflated. Often they waste time and energy trying to save face or plotting revenge. Additionally, it is not always easy to determine another person's true feelings. A person who lives by the opinions of others squanders his valuable mental resources and is not qualified for inquiry.

The Solution - Inquiry into *Isvara*

If I take time to analyze the factors involved, I will clearly see that demanding respect from others cannot bring comfort or satisfaction, even if I am a highly accomplished person. First, I should investigate the basis of the factors that motivate me to demand respect from the world. The answer is that I believe that I am the author of my actions, the producer and owner of my gifts and skills. But is this true? What did I actually create? It is clear that I did not create my body. I appeared here one fine day encased in a fleshy meat tube by no effort of my own. I did not create my sense of individuality either: it came along with the body and the world in which the body exists, a world that I definitely did not create. Certain tendencies - skills and abilities - sprouted from within me by no will of my own. I can utilize them, but I cannot claim authorship of them. Whatever achievements I claim depended on opportunities that were provided by life itself. I did not cook them up. I just happened to be in the right place at the right time. How I got there is a mystery.

If I am a reasonable person, I should conclude that whatever talents, skills and gifts I enjoy are given by *Isvara*. I should appreciate them as such and make use of them or not, without fanfare. They should speak for themselves. Whether or not they are noticed and appreciated by others should not concern me. A flower in a vacant lot in a slum blooms unnoticed for no other reason than it is its nature to bloom. Pride ceases to be important when I see that it is a false value that does not work.

Once I understand the psychology of pride I should remain alert, and when it raises its ugly head I should examine my thinking dispassionately without a sense of guilt or self-condemnation. Why do I care what people think? I feel inadequate. Is it true that I am inadequate? Will the attention of others remove my sense of inadequacy? Even when I am acknowledged by people, the sense of satisfaction it engenders does not last and I am forced to seek approval once more. When does it end? Is it reasonable to claim these things when it is clear that I did not create them? Is this *samskara* real? Who is this for? It is for my ego. Is my ego real? It is not real, because it disappears when I look into it. Why do I invest so much energy in something that is not even real?

I cannot just drop my prideful ego, but by meeting it head-on I see how pointless my expectations are, and after some time this *samskara* loses its power to disturb my mind. The habit of seeking approval eventually winds down and I become an uncomplicated person.

2. Pretension, Affectation

Pride is based on real accomplishments or abilities, but pretension is self-glorification without a cause. I want to give the impression that I am something I am not. If I dress like a prince, my bank account is overdrawn and I am dodging bill collectors, I am pretentious. If I claim to have a country estate in the South of France when I live in a rent-controlled apartment in the ghetto, I am pretentious. If I can't answer the doorbell without first tidying the living room for fear that someone might think I am a messy person or I cannot appear in public in a mismatched outfit without my lipstick and every hair in place, I am a poseur. If I have done no meaningful spiritual work but wear orange robes, shave my head, carry a staff and wander around spiritual centers with a beatific smile pasted on my face to convince others of my mystic attainments, I am not a *mahatma*. I am a phony.

All unhealthy *samskaras* stem from the same basic reason, the understanding of which should never be far from my mind. It is: I do not feel good about myself. I cannot accept myself. I want to be different. I am so extroverted that I cannot see my own psychology and take responsibility for it, so I rely on others to do what I should be doing for myself, i.e. make me feel good. I need to impress people so they will validate me.

This is a particularly difficult problem, because I don't even have the satisfaction of knowing that what I am saying about myself is true. I am therefore committed to falsehood and find myself in direct conflict with truth. This attitude is particularly vexatious because there is no way to compel others to respond favorably to my lies. Because I badly need others to respond and because at any time my lie may be exposed, I am subjected to a surfeit of stress. To make it work I need to be very alert, keep all my friends apart and have a very long memory. There is a belief that *karma yoga* – leaving the result to *Isvara* – works in this situation, but it doesn't, because *karma yoga* assumes that one's values are in order. It does not get your values in order. It is not to be used to mask a psychological problem or manage an *adharmic* situation.

Obviously, a mind practicing untruth is too agitated to dispassionately inquire. It is telling me that I am unacceptable, and Vedanta is telling me that I am acceptable both as a *jiva* and as awareness. So there is a glaring disconnect between what I am pursuing – validation for a part of myself that is not even real – and what I say I want: freedom from the suffering produced by my identification with that unhealthy part.

The solution is to admit the problem, accept scripture's idea of who I am and be willing to consider others' views because they see what I don't see about myself. Or I should have the confidence to discount their views because I know that they are projecting a false image onto me owing to their own lack of clarity.

There is no learning and no growth for poseurs. I cannot solve even the basic problems of desire and anger if I am a proud, pretentious person. Without it I become a simple individual capable of honest self-examination.

3. Non-Injury

I have a value for non-injury because I do not want to be hurt. It is the same for all living beings. Non-injury is a nuanced value difficult to apply, owing to the apparent nature of the world in which we live. Three categories of injury prevail: actions, words and thoughts. The most obvious expression of an injurious action is physical violence.

A common expression of non-injury favored by spiritual types is vegetarianism. The argument is: although life eats life, human beings are not in the same choiceless category as animals, whose food is dictated by instinct. We are self-conscious and endowed with free will, and since there are many means of survival, we are free to choose a non-ambulatory food source. Although plants are living beings, they are not conscious as animals are, so eating grains, fruits and vegetables is morally superior to killing conscious beings. Swami Dayananda, a great champion of vegetarianism, says, "To bring meat-eating in line with *dharma* I would have to kill my prey bare-handed, without the assistance of weapons, thus exposing myself to the possibility of becoming some animal's dinner." If I am not willing to do this, I am little more than an unethical, cowardly hypocrite "owing to an incompletely assimilated value for non-injury revealed by my failure to risk the possibility of suffering the same result."

For many, vegetarianism is sufficient as far as the value for non-injury is concerned, but the definition of non-injury includes two other types of *karma*: thoughts and words. Words should be truthful and pleasing. White lies are okay in certain situations because compassion trumps honesty. Our sensitivity to physical violence needs to extend to include a careful consideration of the effects of our words on others and the effects of harmful thoughts on our own minds. You may think that your bad feelings are justified by the *adharmic* behavior of others, but they do not punish the offender or make the situation right; they serve only to hurt your own mind.

It is a shame that since the sixties, when hedonistic individualism became acceptable – if it feels good, do it! – society became increasingly disturbed and the traditions of civility, manners particularly, gradually declined. The solution to negative thoughts and actions is to develop an appreciation of the feelings of others because, considering the non-dual nature of reality, there are no others. "Others" is only an idea in an ignorant mind. To develop such an appreciation, I need to look beyond my own needs. Such an attitude is conducive to self-inquiry insofar as both inner and outer conflict is not conducive to self-inquiry.

The psychology: when I feel small, inadequate and incapable of getting what I want, I may resort to violence to achieve my ends. The solution: develop an appreciation for the feelings of others.

4. Accommodation, Commodiousness

To cheerfully and calmly accept any type of person or a given situation – not resigned indifference – is to be accommodating. It is based on a clear understanding that, owing to the law of *karma,* things cannot be different from the way they are. A person's behavior is a consequence of his conditioning and is not subject to will power. People are incarnated to work out *karma,* not to please me. Situations are the result of all the factors in the *dharma* field and are beyond the control of individuals. It is foolish to like or dislike them. All successful relationships depend on one's ability to accommodate to others. Similarly, I cannot be different from what I am, and my situation is the result of my *karma,* so I should cheerfully accommodate my apparent self, not desire it to be different or struggle to change its circumstances. Those who refuse to adjust to reality are constantly disturbed and unfit for inquiry.

To develop this important quality I should learn to appreciate variety, cultivate an attitude of diversity and constantly monitor my mind for a sense of dissatisfaction. When I find myself dissatisfied, I should reduce my expectations. It is helpful to see myself and everyone else as helpless fools or inert objects. I have good relationships with inert objects because I expect nothing of such things. I suffer fools gladly because I know they cannot be otherwise.

The key to accommodation is to respond to and identify with the person, not to their actions. Understand that the person is the self, temporarily bewitched by *Maya*. Try to remember that *Isvara* is behind an angry outburst, a fit of jealousy or a domineering action, and appreciate the fact that if they have no control, I have even less. With this kind of understanding it is easy to become accommodative.

Mechanical reactions stifle accommodation. To be free to respond to the person, I must act consciously, not react like a robot according to my *vasanas*. Swamiji again: "A reaction is a mechanical, non-deliberate behavior, a conditioned response borrowed from previous experiences, one not given prior sanction by my will. That is to say, it is a response which I do not measure against the value structure which I am trying to assimilate, but which I just allow to happen."

Reactions can go against all my wisdom and experience; these factors get relegated to the background and the reaction comes. I may have read all the scriptures of the world, I may be a great student of ethical systems, I may be a professional degree-holding giver of counsel to others, but when it comes to a reaction, my reaction will be just as mechanical as that of anyone else.

Therefore until universal values become thoroughly assimilated, providing a ground out of which right attitudes and actions spontaneously arise, I must consciously avoid reacting and deliberately choose my attitudes and actions.

Want to Be a Saint?

If you are aiming for sainthood, non-injury and accommodation are the minimum requirements. Wisdom and scriptural knowledge are not necessary, only these values. Saints do not consciously hurt others with their words, thoughts or actions. They accept people – good or bad – as they are and have an endless capacity for forgiveness and mercy. They respond to the person, not their actions, because they know that *Isvara* is the doer. This attitude expands the heart.

5. Straightforwardness, Truthfulness

Alignment of thought, word and deed is straightforwardness. Saying one thing and doing another or doing something and saying something else is not conducive to peace of mind and inquiry. Straightforwardness includes not only truthful speech, but thought and actions. Non-alignment fragments the person, subjecting him to a restless mind disturbed by many conflicts.

6. Service to the Teacher

This is a tricky value that requires a lot of discrimination, particularly for Western individualists who, for good reason, are not used to the idea of surrender to anything. Service implies a frame of mind that constitutes surrender of will, subordination of likes and dislikes, a willingness to give without asking anything in return and a general attitude of respect. Service should not be given lightly and given only to a teacher of great integrity who does not ask for it, because she has no need for it. If a teacher demands surrender, she is not a true teacher and the student who surrenders to such a person is asking for suffering. Only the student should benefit from the surrender.

Service is a state of mind that does not require physical action, only the willingness to act. In the ideal student-teacher relationship there is no give-and-take as in other relationships. There is only giving on the part of the student. The teacher is a stand-in for the self and serves by providing an object of meditation for the student. If the teacher is established in the self as the self and has worked out all his personal issues, the opportunity to serve a teacher is the greatest blessing.

I was fortunate to have had a true teacher; the benefits were enormous. It was the high point of my life. My desire for freedom grew by leaps and bounds because I could observe first-hand a free being living free in *samsara*. I was asked to do very little except to be present and alert at all times, and when I needed something, which was exceedingly rarely, my teacher was there for me.

7. Cleanliness

The value of external cleanliness and orderliness is obvious, as it makes life pleasant and brings about attentiveness of mind. Dayananda again: "Even as every day while I go about my business a little dust settles on my skin, some dirt smudges my clothes, my desk becomes littered, my mind gathers dust in my transactions with people. Smudges of envy settle, a spot of exasperation lands, streaks of possessiveness appear and overall a fine dust of self-criticism, guilt and self-condemnation spreads. Each day, until my false identification with the mind dissolves and self-knowledge arises, the mind must be cleaned. What is the detergent for the mind? It is applying the opposite thought. It should be applied even though my negative attitude seems justified by circumstances."

A resentment settles in my mind even though I was legitimately wronged. Allowed to remain, it can build up to hatred. So I deliberately look for reasons to like the person that harmed me. He is liked by others, loved by his wife, takes care of his children properly, gives to charity, goes to church on Sunday. When I look into any other person I will find love. I am capable of loving, and everybody is capable of love. Even a rank criminal has within him the elements of love and sympathy. It may be that his capacity for love is so obscured that it manifests only in the sympathy he shows himself - when he accidentally bangs his thumb with a hammer, for example. But it is there to be discovered. Apparent or not, everyone has saintly qualities - compassion, mercy, love, harmlessness. Therefore to clean the mind of resentment and various dislikes, which will solidify into hatred and other negative feelings, I should deliberately search for those things which indicate humaneness and saintliness. When you do so, attribute the bad things to wrong thinking, bad upbringing or a bad environment. Take it as a blessing that you are not in his shoes. With a similar background you would do the same things. Saintly qualities belong to the self and constitute human nature. Negative qualities are incidental; they come and go.

So when resentment, dislike and hatred towards someone arise, see the person behind the *adharmic* action from an opposite viewpoint and you will discover some sympathy or understanding. Your attitude should be accommodating. In this manner, any resentment, any hatred, is cleansed daily.

Selfishness is perhaps the most common impurity. When I discover that I am caught in non-consideration of the wants, needs and happiness of others, I should deliberately do an unselfish action. When a resolution to clean up unselfishness is backed by an action, it is hard for a selfish *vasana* to perpetuate itself. There are many opportunities every day to put down what you are doing and give a helping hand.

Self-condemnation, like selfishness, is just an impure thought. When something does not go according to plan or I find myself in conflict with a universal value and a feeling of guilt, inadequacy and self-judgment arises, I can counteract it by deliberately bringing self-knowledge to mind: "I am whole and complete, ever-pure awareness." Here is a statement that should be spoken out loud every day that will help to root out negative thoughts about oneself: "The body/mind/sense complex, the doer, which I think is me, cannot be condemned, because all its parts are inert. They do their jobs automatically or at the behest of the mind. It is innocent. The mind is also innocent. It is only an ever-changing aggregate of thoughts in motion, programmed by *vasanas* which are born unconsciously out of unconscious actions and attitudes. It is only an insentient instrument. I cannot condemn it. I cannot condemn an impure thought, because it belongs to ignorance, not to me."

Purifying guilt and regret alerts the mind to further transgressions of *dharma*. If I think I am the doer, regret will arise. If a particular thought is responsible, I am off the hook. Without the emotional disturbance I can address the ignorance that produced the thought. Here is a *mantra* that should be chanted every day:

> "Desire does it. Desire is the Doer. I am not the Doer. Desire causes action. I do not cause action. Salutations to you, Desire. Anger does it. I don't do it. My prostrations to you, Anger. Ignorance caused it. I am not ignorant. Obeisances to you, O Ignorance."

It places the blame where it belongs, and at the same time acknowledging the transgression frees the mind to contemplate the self. If you are fear-oriented, substitute the word "fear" for desire.

Another value that falls under this heading is chastity, which amounts to a respectful attitude toward the opposite sex, not lack of physical intimacy.

8. Jealousy and Envy

One of the most common and unreasonable impurities is jealousy, a pernicious form of duality. It exists because the world is vast, filled with millions of entities that provide myriad opportunities, real or imagined, for self-demeaning, comparative judgments. Jealousy and envy are transformed anger and usually lead to depression. They are produced by a sense of lack brought on by comparison to someone I think is superior in some way to me. It is unreal for this reason: I am never jealous of the whole person, only some aspect. He is more intelligent, beautiful, wealthy or popular than me. The fact that I would like to be like this person shows that there is some sympathy for him. The qualities that invoke jealousy cannot be separated from the complete person. Because the complete person, who is actually the self, can never be completely an object of envy, there is no real place for my bad feelings to attach themselves. Finally, it is also clear that there are certain things in that person that I do not want. Additionally, if I am honest, I will find that I too am not perfect and am the possessor of certain unenviable qualities, knowing which makes it difficult to judge others. If the shoe fits, wear it.

Jealousy is actually an unwarranted reaction to the apparent nature of reality. It is completely without merit. In other words, jealousy is a projection that masks an insufficient appreciation of my own nature and the abundance of good qualities that spring from it. A self-realized person is never jealous, because she is mindful of her fullness.

Although the Bible's statement that God is "a jealous God" means that when you know God you cannot love anything else, many people believe that God is a superbeing sitting somewhere else, who is endowed with certain human qualities, one of which is jealousy. But God is not a person subject to any form of limitation. It is the creator and possessor of everything and, like an enlightened person, knows it is fullness itself. So jealousy and other emotions, positive and negative, do not apply to God.

When I feel jealousy I should apply the opposite thought and nip it in the bud, lest it devolve into *schadenfreude,* delight in the misery of others, a truly despicable emotion. I should think, "I am happy for the good fortune of this person. I admire his good qualities. I am happy that he is happy."

Any negative feeling that is opposed to peace can be neutralized by applying the opposite thought. At first it may seem untruthful to think this way – after all, I really don't feel it! – but a deliberate daily practice will cleanse the mind and prepare it for self-knowledge.

9. Steadiness, Constancy, Perseverance

A consistent effort to achieve a stated goal is required for self-knowledge because self-knowledge is not partial knowledge like worldly disciplines. It is absolute, the essence of all knowledge. Certain actions flow from my commitment to my goal and I should steadily perform them. Most of us are totally resolved at the beginning of any endeavor, but we quickly lose interest when we are confronted with the enormity of the task and seize some pretext to opt out of the required *dharmas*. Steadiness, sometimes called devotion, implies an acute appreciation of the power of *rajas* and *tamas* to distract and cause laziness. To give in to them is to generate a sense of guilt that will eventually paralyze the mind and lead to failure.

10. Mastery of Mind

To value a controlled mind is to understand the way the mind thinks and to bring it in line with the way the self would think if it was a person living in the apparent reality. It means that although the mind is capricious I need not fulfill its fantasies and yield to its caprices. It means that I am the boss, not the mind.

There are four basic ways of thinking, three of which are necessary to understand and master if I want to prepare my mind for self-knowledge:

1. Impulsive. Unexamined thoughts born of instincts dominate the mind. I do what I feel without thinking about it.

2. Mechanical. Thoughts of which I am conscious but have no power to control, because they are produced by binding *vasanas.*

3. Deliberate. Thoughts subjected to discrimination that are accepted or dismissed with reference to my value structure.

4. Spontaneous. Without evaluation my thinking automatically conforms to universal values and my actions are always appropriate and timely. This kind of thinking applies only to those for whom self-knowledge has destroyed binding *vasanas* and negated doership.

Spontaneous thought is not included in this value, because it applies only to self-actualized individuals. If my thinking is impulsive, conditioned or deliberate, I am not a master, but by deliberate thinking the mind can be controlled. Relative mastery is simply alertness (*sattva*) and involves deliberately submitting all thoughts and feelings to rational scrutiny and substituting the appropriate logic whenever ignorance-born mechanical thinking dominates the mind. If I am conscious of my mind, I can learn from my mistakes and exercise choice over the way I think, allowing me to fulfill my commitments to my goal in the face of various distractions and to change my behavior so that it conforms with universal values.

Control of mind, control of senses and single-pointedness are qualifications for inquiry. Mind control is discipline over one's thinking at the level where the thoughts arise, sense control indicates discretion at the level of the senses and single-pointedness is the consistent capacity to stick with the teachings in the face of unhelpful thought patterns – applying the opposite thought, for example. The first two make the mind capable of single-pointedness.

11. Dispassion toward Sense Objects

An extremely important value that amounts to existential maturity, dispassion is defined as a clear appreciation of two hard-to-assimilate facts: (1) the joy I seek is not to be found in objects and (2) life is a zero-sum game. It strips away false emotion created by my *vasanas* and presents the world as an objective fact to my mind. It is also indifference to the results of my actions.

12. Renunciation, Austerity

It would be difficult to find a more spiritually useful value than renunciation. Post-war World War II prosperity has created societies chock to the brim with needy, wanting creatures: "I want what I want the way I want it and I want it NOW!" This attitude, inspired by the wholesale spiritual emptiness of huge populations, has produced an intensity and volume of disturbing thoughts that is unprecedented in human history. The solution: cultivate a value for renunciation. The holy *mantra* of the renunciant is "less is more." The fewer gross and subtle objects I crave and possess, the more peace I enjoy.

13. Absence of Egoism

Because we are discussing the topic of values, absence of egoism is not the complete freedom from the sense of localized "I-ness" afforded by self-knowledge. It is simply recognition of the difference between the ego and the self.

Pride is little more than ignorance of the relationship between the individual and the world. The individual is an ego, a conscious being, brought here to fulfill its destiny. Egoism is an idea of self, purely a notion of separateness. It is born of ignorance and is the capital with which I-ego begins life and which it spends liberally throughout. It amounts to little more than the groundless claim to ownership of various objects, talents and abilities that belong to *Isvara,* not to the apparent individual. For an understanding of this value, refer to the analysis of pride above because pride and egoism are more or less synonymous.

Swami Dayananda presents an interesting inquiry, contemplation of which will make the absurdity of egoism clear. He says: "Although I am graced by free will and have the power to choose my actions, I have no power over the result, which is no more than a possibility among probabilities. The result of any act is the outcome of many circumstances, past and present, known and unknown, which operate in concert. If my strong, skillful arm throws the winning pass in the final seconds of a football game, there are too many material and circumstantial factors coming together for the win to be considered a matter of personal pride. I am creator neither of the football nor of my athletic body. Many experiences contributed to the development of the skill in the arm that threw the football. I am not responsible for the clearing of the pregame rainstorm so the event could take place or for the sharp earth tremor that occurred two seconds before I threw. Nor can I claim credit for the skill of my teammate who caught the winning pass. When pride and ego are examined, they become so silly that humility really cannot be considered a virtue. Humility is simply understanding the world – including myself because I am part of the world – just as it is. Absence of egoism allows me to appreciate all the wonderful opportunities that the world affords, opportunities that provide a source of learning and a chance to shed my ignorance."

14. Appreciation of Time

The objects on which I depend for my happiness are obviously subject to time. To make *samsara* work for me, I need to be willfully ignorant of this obvious fact. Ignorance of it prevents inquiry because it keeps me tied to objects. This value is little more than looking at the downside of the very process of life itself. Birth is wonderful perhaps, but it ceases to be so wonderful when you consider death. And the space between birth and death is no bed of roses either; we are all treated to various physical and psychological pains daily. Today you may be happy, but tomorrow you may suffer. Time is a ravenous mouth, consuming everything, including pain. Nothing can be done about it, so keep your goal in mind. Don't fritter it away. Make conscious use of it to do what can be done. Become a master of time and hasten slowly.

15. Absence of Ownership

This value is similar to absence of pride and absence of ego. Here is another clever analysis by Swami Dayananda. Is the body mine? My mother can claim it, in that it is made out of her flesh. The father can claim it, in that it cannot come into being without his seed. It cannot survive without parents to take care of it. The family has a claim, the society too, the bank that keeps your money safe, for instance. Myriad creatures, including bacteria of all ilk, air, fire, water and earth, the sun and moon and so on all have a claim. At best I am a trustee, a caretaker or a tourist taking up temporary residence as the *karma* for this incarnation plays out. Without the idea of ownership my relationship with objects becomes purely factual, and in the absence of attachment my mind becomes settled and capable of inquiry. *Isvara* "owns" it all.

Two positive values that correspond with absence of ownership are charity and generosity. Spiritual life is about giving, not getting. The heart that gives gathers.

16. Absence of Excessive Attachment to Loved Ones

I am here to add value to the creation; the beings I love are meant to be loved by me. For the same reason that I own nothing and have created nothing, sticky attachment to loved ones is not justified. However, I should look after them in a caring and dispassionate manner.

17. Sameness of Mind in All Circumstances

Based on an understanding of *Isvara*, this value is a variant of dispassion. It is a state of mind that does not swing between elation (*rajas*) and depression (*tamas*). To achieve this state of mind I need to strip my projections from the objects, usually people, including myself, and view them factually. Once subjective feelings are reduced to fact, the mind assumes a stance that makes it easier to appreciate the vision of Vedanta. It is true that Vedanta reveals "facts" to be *mithya*, apparent realities, but to understand what *mithya* means and free myself of it, it is necessary to remove subjectivity.

18. Unswerving, Non-Dual Devotion to God

We refer to awareness as *Isvara*, God, not pure consciousness, in the discussion of values because values are only an issue for someone who does not know who they are, so the devotion mentioned here is not hard and fast self-knowledge. It is an understanding that a *jiva* seeking freedom would do well to assume, as it produces the steadiness of mind mentioned in the last value.

It is *karma yoga*, an attitude of grateful acceptance brought about by seeing *Isvara* as the giver of the results of actions. Like inquiry, it frees the mind of projections and brings it in line with objective reality, making the assimilation of the teachings possible.

19. Love of Solitude

Love of solitude is an obviously valuable value, as one cannot inquire when the mind is connected to and surrounded by other busy minds. Love of solitude is not escapism, because the need to escape indicates an inability to face oneself. An activity that leaves you feeling incomplete when you cannot do it has become an escape. Love of solitude is a mind that enjoys being with itself and is the perfect environment for self-inquiry.

20. Absence of Craving for Company

This is a companion value to love of solitude. A quiet place in and of itself is not intrinsically good, nor is the company of others bad. Fear of people and craving company are not healthy values. The value touted here is a value for a happy, non-escaping mind that enjoys its own company.

21. Constant Practice of Self-Knowledge

In every waking moment, keeping in mind that all I really want in life is freedom and knowing that ignorance of reality obstructs my experience of freedom, is the value indicated here. Furthermore, it includes knowing beyond any doubt that self-knowledge – knowledge of myself as awareness – is the only solution. This conviction should be so firm that *samsaric* goals – security, pleasure and virtue, as discussed in Chapter I – do not turn my head. This value was discussed in the chapter on qualifications as a burning desire for liberation. When this value is assimilated, the next and final values are easy to understand.

22. Resolution, Completion

Excessive *rajas* is the bane of spiritual life. While individuals with *tamasic* minds find it difficult to initiate projects, individuals with predominately scattered (*rajasic*) minds find it difficult not to start projects and then to complete them. Unless you follow through on a resolution, your mind will become more and more disturbed as unfulfilled *vasanas* build up. So it is necessary to have a strong value for completing actions. To master this value, do one thing at a time – no multitasking! Only when a given project is completed do I take up the next. In addition to *karma yoga,* it is necessary to investigate the source of my many needs and plethora of activities, identify it for what it is – a false idea of who I am – and neutralize it with the knowledge "I am whole and complete. Nothing that I do will change who I am. And once I am committed to liberation and understand the value of inquiry I must stick to my practice until I am free."

23. Precaution, Deliberation and Restraint

To correct the inclination to impulsively initiate projects, it is important to value caution. I should deliberately think things through, carefully considering the upside and the downside before jumping in with both feet. Once committed, I should work patiently. In the name of speed and the feeling "I am doing," *rajasic* individuals waste inordinate time and effort on unnecessary actions.

65. "Offering all activities to the Lord, one should direct negative feelings – desire, anger and pride – to Him."

In spite of our best efforts to give up desire, anger, greed and delusion, they may continue to arise in the mind. To address this, Narada suggests that they be directed toward God. Refine the desire to enjoy objects into the desire to know the truth. Desire steadiness in contemplation of the self.

As Shankaracharya says in the first verse of *Sadhana Panchakam,* one should desire to:

> "Study the *Vedas* regularly and put their teachings into practice. Worship the Divine in that manner and give up the thought of worldly things. Wash away negative habit-energy, and examine the defects of worldly excitements. Relinquish your limited identity and claim your identity as awareness."

If you need someone to blame, blame *Isvara.* Nobody wakes up in the morning thinking, "Let's see, how do I want to feel this morning? I think I will be angry. No, I did anger yesterday. I think I will be depressed. And tomorrow I will be envious. Oh, I think jealousy is a good emotion for Friday. Let's do anger on Saturday. And Sunday? Hmm, I'm not sure. I think I will wait until Saturday to make up my mind about my Sunday feelings." *Isvara* is the Causal Body, my subconscious mind, the source of my positive and negative emotions. They arise automatically as I contact objects. Blaming others is not helpful. Making your way successfully in the world is virtually impossible if you hold others accountable for your feelings. Esteeming yourself properly is equally difficult if you continually blame yourself for emotions that are not under your control.

That *Isvara* is to blame, however, does not absolve you of the responsibility to do your *karma yoga* and inquiry. The way out of negativity is spiritual practice, developing healthy *vasanas.* Healthy *vasanas* displace unhealthy *vasanas,* so the more diligently you practice, the more positive the mind eventually becomes. People with predominantly *tamasic* tendencies actually believe that if the world – or *Isvara* – is to blame and nothing can be done to change the situation, they can refuse to exercise their free will and are entitled to lapse into permanent anger or depression. Never believe that objects – a job, a family, the government, etc. – control you. At times it certainly seems as if they do, but objects are not sentient. They are value-neutral, purely projections in *Isvara's* cosmic dream.

If you argue that God will punish you for blaming Him/Her, you are wrong. God is not a big person with likes and dislikes. God is totally dispassionate, a "supreme" being who is completely unaffected by what happens in the apparent reality. This teaching is not meant for devotees with reasonable lifestyles and light *vasana* loads; it is intended for those who are living good lives and doing their spiritual practice diligently but who still find themselves in the grip of intense negativity from time to time. Because negative emotions contradict your good opinion of yourself, the ego needs to deflect the blame to preserve its self-esteem. *Rajas* – the projecting power – rides to the rescue. It is *Isvara's* power to project, and every *jiva* shares it. So although it is good to take the negativity as a gift from *Isvara* and neutralize in this way, scripture recommends blaming *Isvara*. At least in this way your attention stays with *Isvara,* not with the world. When you are puffed up with pride, jealousy, anger or any negative emotion, scold *Isvara*: "Why did you make me like this?" – and get on with your life. If you thank *Isvara* for all your good traits, you can equally dedicate your negative traits to *Isvara* because *Isvara,* not you, created you as you are. Remember, this instruction is meant for devotees at the informal dualistic devotional levels, not for those who are well into the *karma yoga* and self-inquiry stages. Both *karma yoga* and self-inquiry resolve all emotions. Because dispassion is not developed at the introductory stage, this practice is offered.

66. "Transcending the *gunas,* the devotee should act only out of pure love of God and remain perpetually in the relationship of a servant to his master or a lover serving her beloved."

Devotion with Desire

Once we have nourished *Isvara*-devotion by associating it with our desires, we need to further refine it. Initially, *Isvara*-devotion is motivated by the desire to get rid of problems or accomplish worldly goals. But this situation cannot last if I want to evolve. I need to reverse the situation and use worldly things as a means for attaining *Isvara*. *Isvara* may be good for finding a soul mate, landing a dream job or getting the mortgage paid off – in other words, a means for gaining pleasure, security and nourishing a sense of egoism and ownership. But am I willing to renounce these cherished things for the sake of the non-dual love that is the fruit of *Isvara*-knowledge? If I see *Isvara* as a means for attaining worldly ends, discrimination between the eternal and the ephemeral remains inoperative and the freedom of non-dual love eludes me, because without discrimination non-dual love doesn't become manifest, even though it is my nature.

Devotion without Desire

A pure devotee is indifferent to the tug of the *gunas* and is ready and willing to drop the desire for any object for the sake of *Isvara*. The world is the means and *Isvara* is the goal.

> "Be free from desire caused by the three *gunas*. Be free from the hold of duality. Establish your life in *sattva guna*. Give up getting and keeping. Be mindful." (*Gita*, 2:45)

The pure devotee has promoted *Isvara* from an errand boy to his or her be-all and end-all. If your devotion is tainted by *samsara*, you have a list of things you want, and if *Isvara* is on the list, it is probably situated somewhere near the bottom. But this kind of condescending devotion is not real devotion. *Isvara* should be at the top of the list or, better yet, the only entry on the list. When you are about to die, you should be able to say that your life was meaningful because you decided to seek *Isvara*, kept your mind on *Isvara* with a heart that knew no otherness and surrendered the results of every decision to *Isvara*. You should be able to leave this world without regrets and know that you lived free, one with everything, in love with everything.

How do you do this? The verse says to live "in perpetual servitude," which means that you always implement *Isvara's* scriptural instructions. Just as a servant can expect to be protected if he follows the commands of his master, a devotee can expect to attain non-dual devotion if he follows scriptural suggestions. The prohibitions and injunctions in the *karmic* section of the *Vedas* are *Isvara's* instructions. If you don't follow them, you are a devotee in name only. The statement that *Isvara* will take care of your worldly *karma* if you keep your mind on *Isvara* "with a heart that knows no otherness" is a statement of fact, a hard and fast spiritual law. If you want to discover the non-dual love that is your nature and you don't follow this suggestion – *Isvara's* statements are always suggestions, never commands, because *Isvara* cannot deprive you of your free will – you will not succeed. Going to church on Sunday, attending a Neo-Advaita *satsang* or singing a few spiritual songs is not necessarily devotion.

You have to put your money where your mouth is. Devotion is committing oneself to following the values outlined by *Bhagavan*. We do not always succeed, because we are weak. Although *Bhagavan* does not expect perfection from us, He/She expects sincere effort if He is going to live up to His side of the bargain. You inform *Bhagavan* of your intention to be free by following scripture. The squeaky wheel gets the grease.

The devotional schools ignore *Bhagavan's* non-dual statements and interpret the word "perpetual" to mean that the devotee's status can never change, that he is condemned forever to duality. So they remain forever in bondage to *Isvara*, which is not the kiss of death if you know what *Isvara* is, because occasional experiential bliss is not to be scoffed at. Furthermore, pure devotees are always looked after. So is everyone else, but pure devotees don't complain about how they are being looked after as *samsaris* do.

However, life is not quite so simple, because reality is *satya* and *mithya*. Bondage and freedom are not mutually exclusive categories. Reality is a both/and, not an either/or. So you are free as awareness – if you know you are it – and the apparent part of you can be happily bound to *Isvara*.

The *Chandogya Upanishad* clearly says: *tat tvam asi* (you are that). Likewise, the *Kaivalya Upanishad* says:

> "I am that which is smaller than the smallest particle you can imagine and I am bigger than the biggest object you can imagine. I appear as the totality of this amazing variegated universe. I am eternal and I am unborn. I am whole, all-inclusive, all-pervasive, undivided, indivisible Being. I am the Lord of everything. I am all knowledge. I am the very essence of ever-auspicious absolute happiness and the absolute reality behind everything that exists. This is what I am."

So in line with the source texts, we interpret the word "perpetual" to mean "as long as there is ignorance." If duality was the nature of reality, Vedanta wouldn't exist.

Chapter V

The Glory of the Supreme Devotee

SELF-ACTUALIZED NON-DUAL devotees are non-different from *Isvara* and therefore they are a great blessing to the world, irrespective of their lifestyles. In the final eleven *sutras,* Narada returns to the important topic of spiritual practice.

67. "Among the Lord's devotees, the greatest are those who are dedicated solely as intimate servants."

Verses 66 and 67 say that non-dual devotees worship as a servant worships a master and as a lover worships her beloved. These examples are meant to indicate an obedience to the knowledge of non-duality as revealed in the scriptures and an intimate, warm, tender, loving egolessness. This does not mean that only if you express your love in these two ways is your devotion non-dual. It is more accurate to say that non-dual devotees worship "according to their relative natures (*sva-dharma*) and according to the fundamental relationships demanded by the basic roles that society expects them to play (*visesadharma*). In line with this idea, they worship as a slave, wife, friend, parent, passionate lover, forbidden lover, a child – and in other ways. These styles of worship apply to both non-dual and dualistic devotees.

Styles of Worship - Love Games

The emotional patterns we have to work with were unconsciously formed in childhood as we interacted with our parents and siblings, and later as we communicated with the society at large. The following devotional "moods" or attitudes (*bhavas*) purify the heart and bring us closer to God. They convert the negative emotions invariably associated with dualistic worldly love into devotional love. These moods or love games are meant to be practiced consciously in the theater of our relationships.

The Child

A popular *bhava* because we so easily identify with childlike parts of the psyche – the famous "inner child" – this method is based on the universal need of children to love their parents. Love of one's parents is not a particularly noble love, born as it is out of the need to survive. If you are a legal adult but your inner child has not yet become an inner adult, and you would like to grow up emotionally, you can love God with the guileless faith of the child, acknowledging and accepting your state of total helplessness, ignorance, dependence and attachment. You should treat all fatherly and motherly figures as if they are God, which indeed they are, including your own parents, living or dead. Parents, our physical source, make nice symbols of God, our spiritual source. Just as we are part and parcel of them physically, we are part and parcel of God spiritually – "cast in the image of God," our Father/Mother in "heaven." God, pure consciousness, is the cause, and the devotee, the *Jiva,* is the effect. Understanding that the effect is just the cause in a limited form instills confidence in our innate divinity.

Similar to the Slave, which is unfolded below, this love game is considered an imperfect vehicle for God-realization, because it does not, except indirectly, cultivate knowledge of God, leaving the devotee vulnerable to primitive religions and exploitation at the hands of unevolved and unscrupulous religious figures. Ultimately, however, love begets knowledge because the intellect develops natural curiosity for what the heart loves, but in the short run this devotional posture is at best a preliminary step in the soul's long march home. Because this style of worship produces such deep attachment, unless the devotee cultivates understanding of the formless aspect of God through scriptural study and meditation, he or she is in danger of forgetting God's greatness and glory, and merely using God, like a child its parents, to satisfy basic needs.

Mom and Pop

Vatsalya, the parental *bhava,* is considered to be superior to the Child because parental love is tempered with understanding, a sense of duty and responsibility. The precious and profound love of God produced by this mood is balanced and enhanced by an equally deep attempt to probe the mysteries of the Divine through scriptural study, meditation and reflection.

Vatsalya taps the universal need to parent and can be successfully practiced by anyone who has felt the need to protect and nurture a small helpless creature. Children, because of their purity, innocence and guileless bliss, make excellent symbols of God. When the devotee develops this feeling for his or her inner self, he or she shines with maternal or paternal splendor. According to one Indian text, when maternal feelings for God achieve rapturous intensity, this mood is even known to produce mammary secretions in women!

Because it forces the devotee to identify with the mature part of the psyche – the "inner parent" – this mood helps heal negative views of one's parents, which is absolutely necessary for spiritual growth. In fact worship of "the ancestors" is a compulsory part of the *karma yoga* practice.

This *bhava* also teaches the devotee to detach from ideas of guilt, power, fear and punishment associated with God. Calling into questions ideas of reverence and obedience, it also roots out atavistic concepts of low self-esteem and unworthiness associated with God's glory, majesty and grandeur – projections of a primitive religious consciousness. Unlike the child, the mother and father are not moved to awe in the presence of the child. Because they cannot ask favors of a child, this love game negates the tendency to ask favors of the Lord. And, like parents their children, the devotee is enjoined to make any sacrifice for the sake of God.

The Wife

The tie between the husband and wife is the strongest and sweetest in the world, containing all love expressions, particularly sexual intimacy, which is taken to symbolize the union of the devotee and God, the ecstatic wedding of the individual and the supreme self. In this mood of complete identification and attachment, the devotee, regardless of gender, sees God as the husband or wife, to honor and obey in every life situation, even beyond the grave. Just as devoted spouses will gladly suffer for each other, the devotee will suffer any misery on behalf of his or her beloved Husband or Wife.

The Friend

A more common form of worship, one that transforms worldly love into devotion, is *sakya,* friendship, in which equal love flows between God and the devotee. God is seen as a tried-and-true confidante, a close relative or family member, one with whom innermost secrets can be shared. "Henceforth I call you not servants, for the servant knoweth not what the lord doeth, but I call you friends, for all things I have heard of my Father I have made known to you." Those who practice this attitude find their greatest happiness in the happiness of God in others and dedicate themselves to the spiritual welfare of their friends. The relationship between the teaching and the student that anchors the teaching of the *Bhagavad Gita* showcases this kind of devotion.

In this style of worship, a diffident, sacrificing attitude toward God – the Friend – is cultivated. As do close friends, the devotee acutely suffers moments of separation, continually craving God's company, either in the form of a deep experience, through communication and conversation with other devotees and/or by contemplating scriptures, which are God's words. The tender, joyful and playful relationships of nine- and ten-year-old children serves to model this charming mood, which sees God as a dear playmate sporting among His or Her creations.

It is a pity that the modern spiritual world does not appreciate the value of this kind of relationship between the teacher, who ideally should represent the self in the mind of the devotee and the devotee, who ideally should represent the self under the spell of ignorance in the mind of the teacher. It seems instead to prefer the uninformed religious model wherein the teacher assumes the role of the authoritarian parent, and the seeker the role of a weak and obedient child. In fact it would do well to contemplate the following statement from Vedic devotional culture: "The Lord is the devotee of the devotees." Associate with a teacher who does not model this kind of devotion at your peril.

The Slave

The Slave is based on the idea that we're all slaves to our unconscious urges and inclinations. Who isn't chained to physical passions, indentured to selfish feelings, painfully shackled to unforgiving thoughts? The more we strive for freedom, rail and rebel against the injustices of society and aggressively court empowerment, the more we admit our bondage to the unreal.

To convert the feeling of powerlessness into a positive devotional force is the purpose of "*dasya bhava,*" a devotional psychology ultimately leading to self-love and freedom. A service-oriented psychology, the devotee uses it to worship God and Its manifestations, people particularly, with a whole heart, putting his or her life completely in God's hands, seeing himself or herself as God's property, faithfully and diligently executing all Divine instructions with mindless efficiency. Such devotees support and maintain religious, charitable and spiritual institutions, faithfully serve enlightened souls, spiritual teachers and God-intoxicated devotees.

The Slave is considered a sophisticated love game because it develops loyalty and respect, natural feelings in the presence of the Master/Mistress. Secondly, to distinguish God's voice from the many self-serving ego voices requires a quiet mind and keen discrimination. Diligently practiced, this *bhava* quickly reduces ego inflations to rubble.

The Passionate Lover

"Oh, for one kiss from Thy lips, my Beloved!
The thirst of one kissed by Thee increases forever,
His sorrows vanish and he forgets all things but Thee."

About this kiss Swami Vivekananda says, "Aspire for that kiss of the Beloved, that touch of the lips that makes the devotee mad and turns the devotee into God. To the one who has been blessed with such a kiss, the worlds vanish, suns and moon die out and the universe itself melts away into one infinite ocean of love. That is the perfection of the madness of non-dual love." Although the *swami* does not speak of the nature of this "kiss," we need to interpret it to mean the "kiss" of self-knowledge, otherwise all the verse amounts to is a desire for a non-dual epiphany.

A selfless lover eager to gratify his or her beloved is the intriguing model for this *bhava* which characterizes a devotee eager to please *Isvara* by following Its every instruction. It is a difficult love game owing to the difficulty of firming up one's self-knowledge. As ignorance competes with knowledge, the mind blinks on and off and the heart moves from extreme bliss to intense longing. The devotee sees God, the innermost Self, as divinely beautiful and to be worshiped with an affection verging on the erotic. In this style of love, all conventions, reservations, hesitations and personal views are cast aside and an exclusive, potentially jealous, love cultivated. A gargantuan craving for the embrace of non-dual God-knowledge characterizes this mood. Just as lovers locked in the throes of orgasm do not know which body is which, the devotee sees no difference between his or her body and God's body, and all duality disappears, leaving only the sweetness of eternal bliss.

The Forbidden Lover

Operating under the assumption that the more love is obstructed the more it intensifies, this *bhava,* a variation of the Passionate Lover, converts feelings of secrecy and shame associated with love into a positive devotional psychology.

Love of God often awakens in the most unlikely and inconvenient circumstances. When a declaration of love would invite ridicule, condemnation and persecution, taking God as a forbidden lover is helpful. Devoid of outer signs, the Forbidden Lover is a "stealth" psychology through which the love of God grows by inner yearning, silent repetition of the Holy Name, meditation and scripture study. Devotees whose possessive, insecure and jealous spouses can't tolerate their longing for the freedom of non-dual love benefit greatly from this *bhava*.

The Kiss of Self-Knowledge

The previous chapter described a non-dual devotee as one who is firmly established in self-knowledge (*sthitaprajna*) and beyond the *gunas* (*gunathita*). "That devotee who is the same towards praise and blame controls his speech, is contented in any circumstance - even homelessness - and has firm knowledge of the self is very dear to me." (*Gita,* 12:19)

Life is a simple relationship between a conscious subject and inert objects. The firm knowledge that the *Gita* refers to is (a) *brahma satyam, jagan-mithya,* which means that you, the conscious subject, are real and the objects that you witness are apparently real, and (b) *jivo bramaiva naparaha*: you are non-different from consciousness.

The realization of this knowledge in devotional language means "I am love and the objects I experience are non-different from me." In other words, life is love experiencing love. With the discovery of this fact, the devotee is free of the need to look for love in objects, particularly other people. This non-dual love is experienced as a sense of perfect satisfaction with one's self and with the objects that present themselves to the self.

The next verse describes the experience of a fulfilled non-dual devotee.

68. "Conversing among one another with throats choked, hair standing on end and tears flowing, the Lord's intimate servants purify their own followers and the whole world."

To actualize self-knowledge and attain non-dual love is akin to the life of a salmon fingerling born in the mountains of Idaho that journeys five hundred miles down to the mouth of the Columbia River, swims into the ocean where it grows to maturity, then struggles five hundred miles back upstream, overcoming seemingly insurmountable obstacles to return to its birthplace to spawn. When you look back on your life and see that you are the only one of the many thousands of people you have met who have even a vague interest in the truth, you feel a certain sense of satisfaction. And when you think about how at some point you lost interest in pursuing worldly things when everyone around you was still trying to make the world work, your sense of satisfaction doubles. And when, after much seeking, you realized how lucky you are to have understood that the many spiritual paths you tried kept you firmly rooted in the seeking, *samsara,* and from somewhere deep within you summoned the courage to walk away from them, you feel triply blessed. And when you think about how you were miraculously led to Vedanta and you met a kind, qualified, self-actualized teacher, not just an academic, you feel even happier. And furthermore, when you marvel at how the circumstances of your life aligned with your intention and permitted you follow that teacher and at the great care he or she took to teach you, it brings tears to your eyes and a lump in your throat. And when you think about the incredible effort and endless sacrifices you made to keep your mind firmly fixed on the teachings and put them into practice until one fine day you were set free forever, your self-love, self-confidence and happiness knows no bounds. And finally, when you see that this self-confident happiness transforms the lives of others, you know you have done everything that you needed to do and you can die happy.

> "O how wonderful are the scriptures, the scriptures, O how grand is my teacher, my teacher! O how great is this merit, this merit! O how amazing is this joy, this joy!" (*Panchadasi,* Chapter VII)

Swami Paramarthananda says, "I don't know whether to say *Isvara* is great, the scripture is great or the *guru* is great, for they are all mutually interdependent. I can only understand the greatness of the scripture because of the *guru,* and I can only understand the greatness of the *guru* because of *Isvara,* who supplied him. So when I feel like glorifying the scripture, I remember the *guru,* and when I feel like glorifying the *guru,* I think of the grace of God. And when I feel like thanking God, I want to thank myself for having acquired the merit, without which *Isvara* would not have given me all these things. So ultimately, I want to pat myself on the back because this knowledge is bliss. And when I begin to talk about it, I get choked up with emotion."

Even though there is so much evil in the world – cheaters, robbers, rapists and terrorists in the millions – the world remains a fantastic place because of the few non-dual devotees who move around purifying whomever they meet – or those who remain in one place uplifting their communities – because there is no difference between them and God.

The Adequate Devotee

You are a self-luminous being, your radiance unobscured by ignorance and inadequacy. You are the one existence that lends being to every object. You depend on nothing; everything depends on you. Such is the superlative teaching of Vedanta.

The adequate non-dual devotee is a problem-free devotee, who stands alone and wants nothing from the world, not even enlightenment. This devotee is definitely superior to the dualistic devotee caught in *samsara* who feels helpless without God, who begs God for everything, who feels desperate, demanding, inferior, dependent and inadequate. In fact the dualistic devotional world considers independence and adequacy a sign of vanity and pride. The wise non-dual devotee's gratitude to *Isvara* is undiminished throughout his life, even though his debt has been canceled by self-knowledge.

This ever-free person reminds himself of this fact every time he offers "Salutations to the entire teaching tradition (*sampradaya*) starting with *Isvara,* pure original consciousness, cascading down in the form of pure knowledge through Shankaracharya, the most illustrious non-dualist, on down to my own teacher." (*Sadashiva samarambaam, Shankaracharya madhyam, asmad acharaya paryantam, vande guru paramparm.*)

If it were not for this great tradition, I would not have been able to own my freedom. My gratitude to *Isvara* is immeasurable because what we have done together is so great. Is it any wonder that I am emotional?

In the *Taittiriya Upanishad* (part 3, *Bhriguvalli,* verse 10), the non-dual devotee's song is recorded:

> "Bliss! Bliss! Bliss! I am food, the eater of the food and the one that joins these two. I am the firstborn of the true, eternal, immortal self. I am the source of immortality, even prior to the gods. Whoever offers me, surely preserves this knowledge. I am the food that eats the one that eats the food. I am self-luminous like the sun. The one who enjoys this understanding attains the aforementioned result: Bliss! Bliss! Bliss!"

And in the *Taittiriya Upanishad* (*Shikshavalli,* verse 10):

> "I am the initiator of the tree of the universe. My reputation is as high as the Himalayas. I have been elevated to the holiest state and beyond the holiest state. I am the most excellent, self-luminous, immortal being. I am a sunlike power and immeasurably wealthy, refulgent with divine intuition. I have

attained true knowledge and become imperishable and immutable."

When these rare people meet, they share their joy like people who have won the lottery. Imagine life without them, a world without hope, full of billions of dull *samsaris* who live and die without contributing anything. As embodiments of non-dual love they make life worth living, indeed they make it glorious!

69. "They make holy places holy and our lives auspicious. They justify the scriptures."

Dualistic devotees leave their sins in the holy rivers, but non-dual devotees purify the holy rivers of the sins of others – because they are non-different from God. Whatever they do blesses the world. Their dwellings become pilgrim centers. Their lives lend credence to the scriptures.

70. "The non-dual devotee is totally absorbed in God."

A *samsari* keeps everything in his heart except *Isvara,* but a non-dual devotee has nothing but *Isvara* in his heart. So when the devotee moves from place to place, it is *Isvara* moving from place to place, uplifting everyone he or she contacts. His physical body is sacred because the Lord is fully actualized in his heart. No veils of ignorance or egoism obscure the love. A dualistic devotee may say, "God is in me," but a non-dual devotee is *Isvara* through and through; there is no "in" and no "out." He says, "*Isvara* is me and I am *Isvara*."

71. "Their ancestors become joyful, the gods dance and the earth is protected by a good master."

Although my mother and I loved each other, we never saw eye-to-eye on any topic. I always came up short in her eyes. She was most relieved when I left home and struck out on my own, but when I returned with the knowledge of who I was she became humble, without even knowing why, and welcomed me back with open arms. My teacher, who was like a magnificent father, bent over backward to give me a hand in life. I never sought recognition but became very popular. Even the "gods," the forces that control the senses and mind, made my senses more acute and my mind brilliant. And the earth was happy too because I lived so simply I hardly made a mark, and at the same time I reclaimed broken and damaged furniture, relieving her of the need to produce trees.

72, 73. "There are no distinctions among non-dual devotees in terms of social class, education, physical beauty, family, occupation and so forth, because inwardly they are all equal in the sight of the Lord."

All non-dual devotees are equally great regardless of their status, appearance, education or occupation. As Shankaracharya says in *Manisha Panchakam,* "He or she may be a learned Brahmin or an outcast, no matter. The indwelling self that shines distinctly in all three states is the same in one and all, irrespective of caste, creed or kind. The Great One who inculcates this knowledge is the real preceptor."

These people are found in all walks of life and respond to the world according to their predominant *guna,* which is usually *sattva.* Some are active and travel around the world teaching, others remain unknown, eschew society and live like hermits. Some remain in their professions and live the family life. There is no rule. Irrespective of their circumstances, there is no difference between them. Yes, *samsaris* belong to God too, but if you associate with them you don't get close to God, because they cling to a sense of "I" and "mine," which reinforces your sense of duality. If you associate with and revere wise non-dual devotees, you are worshiping the self and will be drawn ever closer to the self in understanding and love.

The following *sutras* wrap up the teaching. They give a few common-sense tips to dualistic devotees, particularly inquirers studying scripture, who want to lose their sense of separation.

74. "Don't argue."

This piece of good advice is intended to warn inquirers to only offer their "wisdom" when it is solicited. The *Bhagavad Gita* says, "Let not the wise unsettle the minds of the ignorant." Scripturally sophisticated but immature people with low self-esteem who are afflicted with *rajasic* competitiveness invariably want to be seen to be intelligent and knowledgeable; they always think they are "right" and take great pleasure in correcting, convincing and guruing others. Ideas put forth from this state of mind lead to arguments, which nourish duality.

Enlightening discussion in which the truth is the only winner is possible only when the conversants are extremely mature. If your sole motivation is to win and you are convinced that the other person is wrong even before you have heard their arguments, you will only generate emotional heat, not light. People walk away happy and satisfied from healthy discussions. Contentiousness only breeds anger and bitterness, not friendship. If you want to cultivate a spiritual friendship, avoid talking about sex, money and religion, and strive to build bridges, not create chasms. Everyone knows what words push people's buttons. Avoid them and seek non-threatening words. Egos tend to be very sensitive and are easily upset. Be mindful.

Approach *satsang* with humility, mutual respect, intellectual honesty and a willingness to be wrong. Speak calmly and unemotionally, and give the other person the opportunity to speak without interruption. Don't distract yourself by planning a counter-argument while the other person is still speaking. If you are unsure of your point of view, be willing to discuss the topic later; don't express half-baked ideas. If you see a discussion leading into argumentation, drop out even if the other person thinks they won. Speech control (*vak tapas*) is one of the most important spiritual practices (*dama*).

Argumentative, opinionated people with a chip on their shoulders are a dime a dozen. Even if you say that it is a hot day when the temperature is in the nineties, they will beg to differ. Contrariness begins early when a child starts to individuate and often becomes hardwired – you say yes, I say no. If at all you communicate with contentious people, formulating your statements in the form of questions disarms them. They think you are humble and may actually be willing to communicate.

75. "Argumentation leads to excessive entanglement and resolves nothing."

Once we get into an argument on a particular topic, each person winds up trying to establish his or her view by giving a lot of reasons and examples, which in turn become fodder for further disagreement. So instead of resolving one issue, we are confronted with a second and a third issue. It is like the Second World War, which started between Germany and Poland, and eventually spread around the globe.

Even in Vedanta, where you would think people are only concerned with truth, you find this problem. The rope/snake metaphor, which is meant to illustrate the distinction between *satya* and *mithya*, has spawned many different interpretations: the self doesn't exist, the world doesn't exist, the *jiva* doesn't exist, *samsara* doesn't exist, etc. Every Vedantic Tom, Dick and Harry has an opinion, and they become completely entangled in argument, each seeking to have the last word to prove how spiritual and wise they are. There is no last word when you have this mentality.

76. "Respect revealed scriptures and follow their suggestions."

The *Bhagavad Gita* is an ideal devotional scripture because it gives a clear roadmap for developing devotion: the four types of devotion and the five stages of devotion.

77. "Patiently waiting as the mind clears of emotionality - distress, desire and accomplishment - invest your time in noble pursuits."

Time is short. If we don't intelligently reduce our obligatory duties, simplify our primary relationships, forego gratuitous transactions meant to make us feel good and trim our possessions, there will never be time to grow spiritually. Simplifying one's *karma* does not immediately simplify the mind. It will suffer an emotional hangover as the *vasanas* associated with our *samsaric* lives continue to bedevil us. *Karma yoga* is the solution for purifying the emotional remnants of our past actions. We need to see them as the play of duality, take them as a gift from God and move on. We need to "skillfully abide in equanimity, viewing success and failure alike as we do what has to be done without concern for the results. Unfortunate are those whose minds are held hostage to the results of their actions." (*Gita,* 2.48-50)

Emotional Hangovers

Happy events linger in the mind and generate the desire for more. Painful events linger and create aversion lest they happen again. Unfulfilled desires cause us to plan ceaselessly and keep the mind away from the Lord and from what needs to be done in the present. Unless we tackle these *vasanas,* there will be no time for inquiry. *Karma yoga* is time management because it purifies desire and fear, the creators of time. Self-knowledge only dawns in a contemplative mind. Without self-knowledge, non-dual love eludes us.

78. "Cultivate the virtues: non-injury, truthfulness, cleanliness, compassion and faith in non-dual teachings."

Simply chanting the name of God is helpful, but it will not deliver the devotee to the supreme abode: non-dual love. Rather than condemn ourselves for our character faults, we should develop the virtues listed here and elaborated above in the commentary on verses 62 and 63, particularly non-injury in "thought, word and deed." Non-injury, the Golden Rule, is simply appreciating fact that I should not do to others what I would not want them to do to me. Devoutly practiced, it removes conflict.

79. "Those who are free of doubts should constantly and wholeheartedly worship the Supreme Lord."

Does this verse mean that someone whose mind is pure should forgo everyday activities, sit alone in silence and keep the mind locked on the self?

Work Is Worship

Ritualistic worship is usually considered to be attending church, burning a candle or lighting incense, offering flowers, telling the rosary or physically prostrating at an altar. But this verse recommends *karma yoga.*

Karma yoga is devotional *yoga.* It is simply love for one's self in the form of the creation. The love you have for life is not self-created. It is not "your" love. It is consciousness, which is love loving in you and through you as you. In the case of *karma yoga,* the self, under the spell of *Maya,* thinks it is a person with love - which is just willing attention - to invest in objects, and because this does not work, the attention it invests in life in the form of action needs to be offered back to the creation in the same spirit in which it was given - to complete the cosmic cycle.

Consecration

Karma yoga is also knowledge *yoga* because to meaningfully worship life with my actions I need to appreciate the non-duality of reality. The love in me for objects is simply the self loving through me, misdirected toward objects. But is it misdirected? If I understand that reality is non-dual, aren't all the objects appearing in me - my life and everything in it - only me? Therefore are not all the objects worthy of worship? Worship is not supplication, it is appreciative love. I am grateful for what I have been given, my self in the form of the creation, and I offer my actions to the creation with an attitude of gratitude.

Karma yoga unwinds the Subtle Body's grasping, fearful orientation. This unconscious stance is there the moment an impulse to act arises and it is present with every thought, feeling and action. It is there when actions fructify, a constant silent companion. To shift a lifelong orientation to its opposite is hard work, a war with the ego. Consecration simply means thinking of the self, reminding yourself of your purpose here, invoking an attitude of gratitude to go with every action and then doing what is required without attachment to the results. When the impulse to act is met directly in this way, it is impossible to perform self-insulting actions or actions harmful to others. We cause injury only when we are unaware of what we do. Nobody becomes more conscious, because consciousness does not change, but we can become more aware of our limited orientation and the unwanted results it produces.

A Gift from God

Life is nothing but the fruits of one's actions after they have wended their way through the *dharma* field. To complete our understanding of the *karma yoga* attitude we need to take what happens as a gift from God. A nice model for this idea is temple worship. A devotee brings an offering to the temple, hands it to the priest who offers it to the deity and returns it consecrated. The devotee is free to do with it what he sees fit, usually distributing it to the beggars waiting outside the temple.

Peace of Mind

Taking what happens as a gift is fine as long as what happens is what we want, but what should I do when the *dharma* field gives me something that I don't want? Should I become angry and reject it? No, I should take it as a gift. Worldly people are happy when they get what they want and unhappy when they don't, but *karma yogis* are happy when they get what they want and when they don't because their goal is peace of mind, not the ephemeral joys that come from objects. How does this work?

The *vasanas* appear in the Subtle Body as likes and dislikes. Likes and dislikes, attractions and repulsions, fears and desires are the enemies of the *karma yogi*. *Karma yoga* is intended to neutralize them because they continually agitate the mind, making it unfit for discriminative inquiry. The *dharma* field is a university meant to teach us who we are. We do not graduate until we have learned our lessons. It instructs by delivering the fruits of our actions. As my wife, Sundari, says, "A *karma yogi* knows that experience is a decaying time capsule meant to deliver knowledge." Results never last, but the knowledge hidden in experience leads us to the self. So when something happens, irrespective of whether it is what we want or not, we are meant to welcome it and learn from it. In this way the likes and dislikes are neutralized and the dispassion necessary for inquiry develops.

Converting even the most mundane and unconscious activities into a prayer is *karma yoga*. Think like this:

> "Whatever I do, I do for you, my self, my essence. You move my mind to drive my body to do your work. My body is your temple and my heart the altar on which you sit dispensing

your love. You digest my food, draw my breath in and send it forth. The enjoyment of my senses is born of their worship of you. Everything I see, hear, smell, taste and touch is you. When I speak, you speak through me. When I sleep, I am one with you. Whenever I walk, I am walking in you toward you, my destination. I love my family and my friends because they are you. Their love for me is you loving me through them."

80. "When glorified, the Lord swiftly reveals itself to devotees and allows them to know him as he is."

If you are a dualistic experience-oriented devotee you will take this verse to mean that when you do some kind of devotional practice – prayer, meditation, *yoga,* etc. – the Lord will appear in the form of some sort of epiphany tailored to your particular need. *Isvara* is all-powerful, no doubt. If It can create the entire universe, appearing as some kind of subjective experience is a small matter. Epiphanies, however, are only as good as the devotee's interpretation of them, and even if they are considered to be enlightenment, they don't last. Usually devotees imagine that they are special because God has chosen to appear to them, and they often develop into piners and whiners because a God that appears has the knack of disappearing as well. And usually, epiphanies don't give clear knowledge of God, because the devotee is so overwhelmed emotionally by the vision that his or her intellect is obscured and the knowledge of God's nature and the devotee's identity with it doesn't take place. At best epiphanies are a brief introduction to non-duality. In any case a spiritual experience does not erase lifetimes of subconscious tendencies, so the devotee goes right back to the humdrum experience of his *samsaric* existence.

So this level of devotion needs to evolve to the point where the devotee's vision of the Lord is always immediately available. And this is only going to happen if his mind is pure enough to see every experienced object – which is always available as long as the devotee lives – as *Isvara.* The *Gita* speaks of this kind of experience: "You cannot see me with this ordinary eye of yours. I shall give you a divine eye to see my divine power." (11:8) The "divine eye" is the inferential "eye" of the non-dual scriptures, which is the firm knowledge "I am limitless, non-dual, ordinary, formless awareness."

81. "Devotion is the most precious possession of a sincere person."

A sincere person is someone honestly dedicated to attaining non-dual love.

Which is greatest of the three levels of devotion: devotion to a remote, indirectly experienced God, devotion to a vivid and directly experienced God or devotion to an imperceptible God known to be non-different from me?

The first two types of devotion are important stepping stones, but devotion that manifests as firm knowledge of God that is beyond form – myself, awareness – is the greatest because it alone liberates. As it says in the *Kaivalya Upanishad*:

> "After discovering the self which exists in all beings and in which all beings exist, one reaches pure original awareness [the self beyond the reflected self]. There is no other means."

Liberation is only possible through the knowledge of absolute reality. Neither God in one form nor God in many forms is absolute, because both come and go. Absolute reality is pure, limitless, attributeless, universal awareness alone: *satyam jnanam anantam brahman. Satyam* is pure being, or existence. *Jnanam* is pure knowledge, not the relative knowledge of objects that occurs in the Subtle Body. *Jnanam* is the consciousness and the intelligence underlying the manifest universe. It is the knowledge that is the very essence of awareness, the knowledge that is the very essence of being, for in the absence of this "knowability" nothing can be said to exist. *Anantam* is limitlessness, fullness. Absolute awareness is infinite and eternal. It is that because of which and within the scope of which everything in existence obtains. It is all-pervasive, but even the word "pervasive" is not exactly right, as it implies duality. The self's eternality is not an unending duration, but beginningless existence. It has always been, is now and will always be beyond the limiting parameters of space and time.

To use the language of the *Bhagavad Gita* (15.17), "Different from the changing and the unchanging 'selves' is supreme, pure, original awareness, which pervades and sustains the Macrocosmic Causal, Subtle and Gross bodies. It is the imperishable Lord."

82. "Although love of God is one, it manifests in eleven forms: reflecting on God's glory, appreciating God's beauty, worshiping God, remembering God, serving God, communing with God as a friend, caring for God in a parental way, interacting with God as a lover, surrendering everything to God [especially doership], absorption in contemplation of God and cherishing separation from God."

Love of God is one because reality is only God loving God. However, it can be expressed in various ways, according to the temperament of the devotee. All (see Love Games above) except the last requires no explanation. It is a perverse devotion in which the devotee imagines himself to be separate from God to enjoy the feeling of absence in separation, just as family members who quarrel continually miss each other when they are apart - absence makes the heart grow fonder.

83. "So it is universally declared by great Vedic teachers who share the same views on the topic of devotion."

The ideas in these verses are completely in harmony with the source texts of the Vedic tradition, which are revealed knowledge, not personal opinions. No *jiva*-inspired teaching is free of defects, no matter how famous the *jiva*.

Hinduism has many schools of thought which are little more than the personal views of great sages, like Kapila (Samkhya philosophy), Kanada (Vaisheshika philosophy), Gautama (Nyaya philosophy), Patanjali (Yoga philosophy) and Jaimini (Mimamsa philosophy). In his commentaries on the second chapter of the *Brahma Sutras,* Shankaracharya refutes them all in light of the teachings on liberation found in the *Upanishads.* Likewise, the *Agama*-based devotional schools - Shaiva, Shakta and Vaishnava - are unsound, because they are human literary works. Selected teachings are useful, but the core teaching should be Vedic.

Traditional teachers take great pains to avoid personal views and teach in a manner that is consistent with the *Vedas,* which are based on an infallible analysis of experience, common sense and reason. In every case, the teaching is: *karma yoga* plus *upasana yoga* plus *jnana yoga* leads to freedom and non-dual devotion.

84. "Anyone who has faith in these auspicious teachings will attain non-dual devotion. Indeed he or she will attain unconditional love."

These Vedic teachings, initiated by Dakshinamurthy *Isvara* and given by Narada, are most sacred, holy and auspicious. *Isvara* is "the sanctifier of everything sacred and the most auspicious of auspicious beings, the undecaying Lord of everything." Whatever *Isvara* says will come to pass. The scriptures are *Isvara's* words. The devotee who follows them with complete faith will certainly attain his or her heart's desire: unconditional, non-dual love.

Om Tat Sat